Sipping Tea with Buddha and Christ

From the lights of Shanghai to the shores of Hong Kong, the rainforest of Guatemala to the crust of Vietnam -- one woman's fight to hold onto her faith without abandoning her heart.

Alexa Benson-Valavanis

Just This Press, Inc.
California

Copyright © 2013 Alexa Benson-Valavanis

All rights reserved in all media.
Published by Just This Press.
First Edition

Author's Note:

The events in this story are real although creative liberties have been taken regarding description, time and location.
Most characters have fictitious names, and identifying characteristics are composites for creativity's sake and brevity. Everything else written is based on actual people and events at the mercy of my messy napkin notes and frayed memory. I can tell you, within the fact and fiction, this story bears my heart and soul.

Copy editing by Leslie Layton
www.chicosol.org

Book design and editing by Kim Maynard
www.kimbilt.com • typwiz@gmail.com

Cover by Caitlin Schwerin
www.caitlinschwerin.com

ISBN: 978-0-9893686-0-5

www.alexabensonvalavanis.com

Printed in the United States of America
10 9 8 7 6 5 4 3 2 1

For Melinda Lee

*She is the sun
And I the moon
for I have life alone
but it is dark without her.*

Acknowledgments

To my mother and father, it was your unconditional love that guided me when the light in my own heart was dim. You made each word that has fallen on these pages possible.

To my twin sister, Alisha, I've written this story to honor my journey but also yours. Your laughter and love has been present every day of my life.

To Leslie Layton, you've spent countless hours editing the work all the while mentoring me as a writer. There are no words to thank you.

To Kim Maynard, you made it possible for others to hold my story. You are so talented. I am forever grateful.

To Tharyn, my big brother, thank you for allowing your brilliance to flow into this work -- so that the world might see it too.

To Scott Wyman your wisdom and teachings gently guide me.

It cannot go without mention that the desire to share my story came from a wish to honor, all those (LGBTQ+) who have died, far too soon, simply because of the way they were born. The deaths are too numerous to count, and would so drastically fall short of honoring even one of the lives taken or lost because of fear, hatred or pain. This story is for each of you.

To the rest of the support I pulled from, at the edge of many nights, Melissa & Mike, Katelyn, Kyleigh, my grandma, Missy & John, Barrett & Ashley, Paula, Doug & Zinita, and my little loves -- Braden, Blake, Beau, Emersen, Hudson, Lauren and Sloan -- your love and support has been a source of strength.

To all those who are not listed but who rest gently in the arms of my muse and my heart, thank you.

For every memory made and shared within this book there was a moment on earth. For all of that time, I am grateful to God.

Ultimately my gratitude must begin and end with Melinda, my great love, my greatest friend -- my wife.
It is because of her love that I survived to share this tale.

In Memoriam
William Valavanis, my beloved Papou

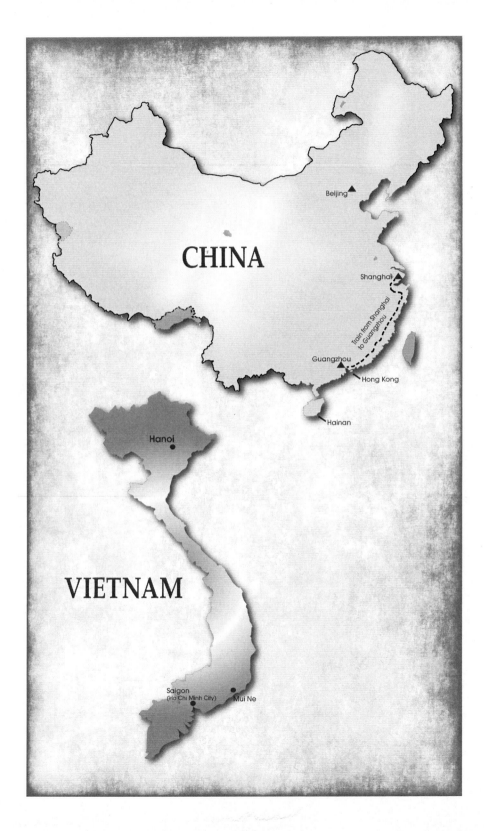

Part One

If we are to lose any part of ourselves to love may it be our suffering.

A Third Way

The tears were not from sadness. It was the sheer magnitude of uncertainty which forced little drops of salt water to the corners of my eyes.

It was sometime during the fall of 2004. I was staying at a friend's place while he trekked through the Guatemalan highlands and held medical clinics for those in need. He traveled to places long since forgotten by modern news headlines and foreign aid.

The needs Dr. Godwin Orkeh found were more than what he could meet, nevertheless, he worked, day after day, helping those he could.

As I took my morning walk to the chicken bus stop, I imagined making that kind of difference in the world. A sleepy dawn held the fierce orb as it cut through the clouds and cast deep shadows on the mountainsides of San Lorenzo el Cubo, Guatemala.

I heard nothing but the birds above and the slight stir of distant villagers. My thoughts were loosely knotted to the stillness of my surroundings as my eyes absorbed the bold colors donned by the Latin rainforest.

On the way to the bus stop sat the San Lorenzo el Cubo town square. It was decades if not centuries old, although it's difficult to determine the age of anything in Guatemala. Gravity and the sunshine work overtime here.

At one end of the town square slouched an old basketball court and its lazy rim. Straight across from the hoop crouched a rectangular pool that housed three concrete basins. This is where the Mayan women conducted their daily ritual of washing clothing.

There was a Catholic church in the far corner of the square with its brightly yellow painted colonial face peeking out. It appeared to be grinning. I, too, was smiling, as I'd longed for silence this morning and was grateful for its company.

As I had each morning since my arrival in Guatemala City from San Francisco, I sipped a lukewarm Nescafé and nurtured fond memories of the sweet caramel macchiato I'd grown to love from the green and white mermaid in the states. Alas, with no Starbucks in sight, I had the quiet to sip on.

Then, without warning, the air in front of me vanished. I felt the cold sharp blade of a machete against my neck. My mind formed a list of the things I was cognizant of the seconds prior to the machete. I have no idea what the point or purpose of forming the list was, but it arrived, uninvited. It was short and concrete.

It was a Saturday. I was walking to catch a bus to Antigua. I was on my way to the store to get items for my risotto. I was walking to the same chicken bus I'd taken numerous times before, uninterrupted.

That was it. That was the list I could form. I watched the coffee fall from my shaking hand. I didn't attempt to stop the warm brown liquid from hitting my sandals. In slow motion the coffee hit the dirt and splattered on to my toes. I looked up. The face holding the machete was as cold and round as the moon.

I know now that things slow down in moments of shock. The brain must process differently with adrenaline racing through the veins. The stranger and I stood there connected by the blade of his machete against my neck and the matching chocolate brown of our eyes. We exchanged movements.

It was a dance I'd never seen before nor imagined I could know. Yet, somehow, I knew to move. *Move. Move. Keep moving.* There was a voice, emerging from deep within me, telling me to freeze, but somehow I knew not to trust it. I kept moving.

Who will call my parents? It was the thought which proved death was near. I felt a warmth drip down my spine. Then, almost instantly, a chill took me over as I stood there in the bright Latin morning light. I dropped my backpack. *What was the value of anything, save oxygen, in a moment like this?*

Certainly, a part of me assumed that offering my belongings to this stranger would conclude our dance. But as I stepped away he stepped toward me. *What could he want now?* Everything of value was there, offered, no questions asked. I was a guest in his land and had made my offering.

Adrenaline tore through my unprepared vessels. It was like waking from a nightmare with heart pounding, but instead of the relief that follows the realization of a dream, I was flooded with adrenaline. It wasn't a dream. This was happening. Fight or flight. *But how could I do either?*

Without explanation I recalled a story I'd heard, or maybe read somewhere, about an older man in a dangerous predicament. It was a charcoal gray night in London and the old man was on a walk to the grocery store.

The weatherman had promised rain, so he carried his reliable black-and-white dotted umbrella on the journey. He made a mental list of items he needed as he walked. Since the rain refused to come, he used the little fabric cane to walk with. He was content, and his whistling was proof of it.

At the market he shopped quickly and left, still anticipating a storm. A few blocks from his house he heard footsteps rapidly approaching from behind. The footsteps grew louder. It wasn't long before the man realized he was in serious danger. Three young men were approaching.

In desperation, he turned down an alleyway, not yet realizing it was a dead end. The young men lifted their faces to the sky with laughter when they realized the old man's error.

Certainly he would be robbed or beaten or both. He felt his aged adrenaline rip through his shell. Fight or flight? How could he do either? There must be a third way, he thought. There had to be. But what was it?

When he got to the end of the alley he slowed and turned to face his attackers, then opened his umbrella and started dancing and singing like a mad fool.

The men froze, temporarily amused, and as each second passed the old man sang louder and wilder. The guys were so startled and entertained they left the old man singing in the alleyway, unharmed. He closed the umbrella and starting walking home right as the first drops of rain fell.

So here I stood. *What was my third way?* The stranger with the moon-shaped face grabbed for my arm. I pulled away violently to show my disapproval. I would fight if that remained the only option left between my life and the Unknown.

The distant sound of the birds continued, unaffected. The sun shone, impervious. My screams were gone. The stirring villagers I'd heard earlier during my walk never appeared. The stranger swung his blade toward me. I saw now that he was just a child, seventeen years old at most. *What was he doing swinging a machete at my face?*

Impulsively, I jumped backward and grabbed the backpack again, this time as a shield. With all of my strength I made my shaking arms hold it against my chest. It was a small, albeit solid divide between my body and his blade. *Was this really happening?* Of course it was, yet the back of my brain wouldn't believe it entirely.

Then, out of nowhere, right in the middle of my shock a blue and battered Toyota pickup truck came bouncing along the dirt hillside. The stranger with the round face pulled back as he knew -- seconds before I had that his window had closed. The truck was the local police. *Was this the normal time they came skipping down the dirt road?* The two officers had seen me. They would certainly help.

The man with chocolate brown eyes had already grabbed my bag. I suppose he was not willing to lose the battle completely. He jumped on his bike and peddled straight into the bright green forest.

Within seconds, the police officers pulled up. Without even a nod in my direction, they jumped out of the truck, brandished their pistols, and ran into the woods. The cheerful truck was left running beside me. The silence in the cool forest was pierced with gunshots. I fell to my knees to pray. I wasn't sure what I should say, or how to say it, but I wanted the boy to escape their bullets.

There is no way to tell how much time passed, but eventually the officers walked out of the rainforest with a beat-up purple bike and a worn pair of Nike running shoes in their hands.

They helped me into the truck. I sat squeezed in between them as we drove around San Lorenzo el Cubo looking for a man without sneakers on. This was like looking for a raindrop in the ocean.

A few hours later, the officers dropped me off at the town square in Antigua. It was where the retired yellow North American school bus would have carried me that morning had I taken a longer shower or sipped a second cup of Nescafé at Ochuko's house. I hadn't and it hadn't. Instead, it was these young officers that saved my life.

"*Que le vaya bien,*" they both yelled out of the windows of the truck as they pulled away. "May you travel well" was a phrase I'd heard hundreds of times. It was something Guatemalans said when they parted, whether to walk a block or to leave on a great journey.

My journey, great or not, had nearly ended by a blade carried by a man whose face held the shape of the moon.

In that moment everything I'd been fighting for and against my entire life dissolved. My endless fight to be worthy of God's love ceased. My perpetual struggle to become someone other than who I was had perished. The fear, hatred and shame I'd carried my entire life -- because I was gay -- vanished inside of that single moment underneath the Latin sun, when death came near.

But that moment on a mountainside in Guatemala happens years after this story begins. This story begins somewhere else altogether.

Somewhere Else Altogether

It was the year 2002.

Tonight was crisp but comfortable enough to sit outside, so I was. I leaned against a steady old oak tree in the backyard and pulled out a Marlboro Light from the front pocket of my slightly faded blue jeans.

I felt the earth press its cold chest against my legs and understood for the first time why trees let their leaves fall. The nights of winter can be rough and energy should not be wasted. I tried to imagine the warmth in my stomach and forget the tingling sensation crawling down my fingertips.

I ripped a little brown match from its paper book, and after three attempts, successfully lit the end. I pressed the new flame against the clean round face of the cigarette and took a long drag of smoke into my lungs. For a brief moment, I relaxed.

In the far corner of the sky dangled a slice of the moon, providing just enough light for thinking. I needed time to think. I was tired of getting halfway to a solution in my mind, then surrendering my thoughts to fear. Tonight with the solid oak tree as my witness, I was going to think things all the way through to resolution. After all, I had big decisions about my future to make.

As usual, regret was the first guest to arrive. I was expecting it. Its presence made my shoulders heavy and tilt slightly toward the earth. I made a conscious effort to straighten up against the leafless tree. This gesture of external confidence brought every questionable decision I'd ever made to the foreground of my mind. I could almost smell the memories in my life that resulted in hurt. The list was long.

I thought of Daniel. I thought of Christy. I thought of the little pink heart beating inside of my chest that I'd spent most of my life being ashamed of. The self-induced punishment brought on by conjuring up memories from my past was powerful, but I'd taken this path before. I would not be intimidated by the sour taste of bad decisions.

Instead, I drew strength from the small crack in my bedroom window that let the unmistakably rich sound of Billie Holiday spill into the yard. Lady Day's resilience would help me counter the early guest of regret with good decisions I'd gathered. I lit another cigarette, and with its glow, I fought to illuminate the pieces of my past worth remembering.

Why are good decisions so much more difficult to fetch? I felt the sharp edge of angst crawling its way up my throat. I'd forgotten that regret brings shame along. On this winter night I hadn't prepared for shame. Together, they were crushing my courage into the earth like fresh ground pepper.

How would I ever make the right decision for my future if my thoughts were trapped in past mistakes?

The small space I'd carved out for thinking had officially been hijacked by anxiety, and my heart was racing too quickly to control with internal dialogue. Veins filled with nicotine no longer helped my cause and perhaps never did. I surrendered to the evening without resolve and went into the house to make a cup of tea.

It was cooler than usual tonight, and I felt slightly betrayed by the woolly beige sweater I had on. I stood over the stove to warm a bit and wait for the water to boil.

As I did, I glanced up and noticed the unoccupied microwave and wondered why it never occurred to me to boil water there. I liked the sound of the tea kettle too much to relinquish such a pleasure to convenience, I suppose. The sizzle of moisture against the stovetop began, and before the steam had a chance to press its lips together and whistle, I pulled the tea kettle from the heat.

The moment I dropped the tightly woven bag of leaves into the hot water, the smell of mint began to permeate the living room. I lit an unscented candle and plopped on the couch to read. I still had unmade decisions floating around inside of my head, but a short distraction with fiction might prove useful.

Perhaps then I could decide whether to finish graduate school in this little Northern California city or move to Nova Scotia to become a nun.

These were the two options I'd settled on in Mary Ann's hospital room right before she died. The real root of my restlessness would have to be explored later. Much later -- long after these other decisions had been made.

Nestled on the edge of Nova Scotia overlooking the Gulf of Saint Lawrence sits a Shambhala Buddhist Monastery called Gampo Abbey. I'd read about it in a book about Buddhism I'd found at the local used bookstore.

Graduate school had consumed most of the money I'd saved waiting tables through college, but if I sold my forest green Honda Civic and modest belongings, I could buy a ticket to the Abbey -- to this place where peace bloomed each spring and contentment crackled in the fire all winter long. I longed to hear the sound the ocean made as it crashed against the cliff beside the monastery.

I pulled the monastery admittance forms from the novel I was reading. The papers were folded and tucked neatly in between pages 33 and 34 of Paulo Coelho's tale about a young shepherd's journey toward self. It seemed the fitting book to tuck dreams inside of. I let the name of the American Buddhist, Pema Chödrön, sit on my tongue for a minute. Just holding her name in my mouth seemed to provide a sense of calm.

"The Abbey is a place where you can come to live the life of a monk or nun. You can come here because you wish to live the life of a monk or a nun or because you wish to experience the support of a monastic environment. In any case, it is a place where you can get away from yourself. You might find this quite challenging and quite amazing. You might find it softens you and awakens your heart."

I'd read the opening paragraph of the forms enough times to know it by heart. "A place where you can get away from yourself…"

If only I could do *just* that. Leave graduate school, move to Cape Breton Island and study the ancient wisdom collected by these enlightened ones. I would absorb what they'd learned of God and the world, of mind and soul, of life and death, of the secrets to offering light to the blanket of darkness engulfing me.

I'd seen the modest smiles worn by the holy people of the world -- smiles that certainly contained contentment. *What else could be tucked behind those grins?* I no longer cared which religion I practiced. I wanted to know the truth about God.

In my mind, the monastic lifestyle offered the greatest chance of discovering that truth. The monastery also seemed like an escape from my suffering. I imagined bland meals and chanting. I dreamed of saffron colored robes and peace of mind. I prayed these spiritual warriors would accept me. *Someone just had to.*

At 25, I'd come to my crossroad. The conflict between who I was and who I thought I was supposed to be in order to please God -- in order to be accepted in this world -- was destroying any chance of real happiness.

After more than a decade of trying to guilt, shame and hate myself into not being gay, what was left of me was in pieces. I was terrified of leaving Christianity behind, but something had to change. Either God could love me as I was or I was meant to live without God's love.

I needed to find out. The scale had finally tipped. I was more frightened of a life of endless suffering than a death in Hell.

I kneeled beside my bed in Hill's house and asked, for the umpteenth time, for God's forgiveness. I couldn't remember a time when I wasn't sorry for who I was.

I needed a new start. I hoped to find a place to worship God where His followers didn't reject me as I was. I'd go to Nova Scotia and call God by a different name. Certainly the Creator of all things would not be offended by something as insignificant as semantics.

Of course, if anyone could understand, it was God. So, instead of explaining my decision, I just begged Him to find me at the monastery.

I would be waiting.

Bang. Bang.

Bang. Bang! BANG!!

I shook off the last thought in my mind just in time to realize there was a knock at the front door. It was so late. Come to think of it, it was the middle of the night.

Wait. Come to think of it, I had been lost in thought for the first time in years. I'd been thinking things through. I had made a decision to move.

I wrapped the burnt orange cardigan I had resting on the couch around my shoulders and walked to the front door. My tea was ice cold. I looked at the cable network box on top of the television, and its neon green lights revealed it was 2 a.m.

East Not West

When fate rings -- pick up.

A petite woman with messy blond hair, sun-kissed skin and a whimsical disposition arrived at the front door at 2 o'clock in the morning. The jagged-edged moon was still lingering in the sky, and the hallways of the house reflected its gentle white.

I answered the door just as this light-haired stranger was turning the handle and walking in. In one movement she threw her bag down and walked over to the couch. The hefty black bag wore wrinkles of time. I saw her disheveled clothes pushing out of the far corner where a broken zipper dangled.

Typically the owner of the house bounced to the front door when a knock arrived, but not tonight. Hillary didn't stir. So I was left there with my new decision to become a Buddhist nun and this stranger's messy bag.

Instinctively I asked, "Are you thirsty?" This question originated from the deep female crevices of my Greek mind -- *hospitality first*.

"I'm good," she said as she walked to the kitchen to grab a glass of water.

She knew exactly where the glasses were, and it was instantly obvious she was somewhere familiar.

"Been here long?" the stranger inquired, as if it was two in the afternoon and a perfectly reasonable time to strike up a conversation.

Disarmed and instantly self-conscious, I hastily buttoned the bottom two buttons of my sweater and replied, "I moved in a couple weeks ago, while I finish the last semester of graduate school. Hillary is doing me a favor by letting me crash here. You know Hill? She's so generous. You do know Hill, right?"

My question seemed to momentarily disturb her familiarity.

"Oh, sorry, right, I'm LeeAnn. You are?"

She didn't bother to wait for my answer. She had undoubtedly transported herself back into the middle of a sentence she started, another time, in another kitchen, with a different stranger at two in the morning.

As she wandered around the house settling in, I heard her mention a flight in from someplace far away, but I was lost in my thoughts again. I, too, was somewhere else. I was lost in my thoughts again as if thinking was the easiest thing I'd ever done.

As a Buddhist nun, I'd have to shave my head. What will my scalp look like? I hope I have a decent looking scalp. If not, I'll have that monastic hood up all the time.

Fortunately, it's cold in Nova Scotia, so the hood will be okay. At least I think it's cold. It's Nova Scotia after all -- even those words sound cold. Yes, it will be cold in the morning. I'll have to get up early. Certainly nuns don't sleep in. One must get up early to find God.

What will my family think of this? My family. How will I do in life without them?

Sadness immediately followed the thoughts of leaving my family outside the monastic walls, so I quickly changed the subject in my mind. I chose to fix my attention on sleep, instead.

I offered a barely audible goodnight to the stranger, as I dragged my feet back to the bedroom. I realized the monastery admittance forms were still in my hand. I folded them along their original creases and tucked them back in the novel, then crawled into bed.

For the next four hours, I counted cracks in the ceiling. This time it wasn't thoughts, but sleep which had abandoned me. I'd finally made a decision to move to Nova Scotia and dedicate my life to God, so why couldn't I finally rest a little? All I wanted was a little rest.

In times of uncertainty, the Weather Channel calms me down. I crave the constant reminder that even with the best science and technology on earth, no one can make accurate predictions about tomorrow. Tomorrow is uncertain -- that's just the way tomorrow comes.

I wanted the Weather Channel but it felt selfish to disturb the real-life traveler in Hill's living room with my neurosis. So instead, I pulled the covers to the edge of my chin and waited for the Earth to finish its minuscule rotation before I rose again.

At precisely 6 a.m., I got up. It would have been impossible to stay in bed a moment longer. As anyone who has ever had a sleepless night knows, the seconds tick by at a pace that can easily be confused with backward.

I walked through the hallway and turned the bathroom doorknob with more force than needed, hoping the noise would stir the stranger. After a sleepless night, I'd collected a thousand questions to ask her and could hardly wait for her to get up. Had she said *"Shanghai?" As in China? Could that provide an "escape from myself…?"*

When you're searching, everything new seems to represent a possibility. When you add suffering to that search, almost everything looks like a sign.

Fortunately, I found a shred of patience in my morning rituals. I made tea. I toasted bread and then slathered it with soft butter and strawberry jam. After I ate, I walked outside to sit underneath the oak tree for a while. I practiced breathing and bringing attention to my thoughts just as Pema Chödrön explained. I'd need to be much better at meditation before I arrived at her monastery.

Around 10 a.m., the middle-of-the-night traveler finally awoke. There was something about her worn backpack and clothes thrown about the living room that made all the Paul Theroux travel books I'd read come to life.

I started to question my infant decision to move to Canada and instead dreamed of the other side of the dark blue ocean. Maybe my peace of mind was waiting there.

Hill had been up for hours watching the replay of the Tour de France on her stationary bike with its nose -- and her own -- pressed against the television. Since LeeAnn didn't seem all that captivated by the Tour, I broke the quiet.

"How about a cup of coffee?" I said introducing myself properly, this time with clothes on and a recently showered scent.

"Alright mate," LeeAnn replied. She called me "mate," and the idea that words like that might find a landing pad in my vernacular made my intrigue blossom further.

"There's a good spot on the corner called Bidwell Perk. Do you know it?" I offered and asked in one.

"Oh, you betcha mate. I love that spot."

We left the house almost immediately. LeeAnn didn't require any fuss time for her hair or makeup. She slipped on brown leather flip-flops and was ready to go. *Was it possible she didn't care what others thought of her?* My intrigue started running laps in my head, and I pleaded with myself to calm down.

When we got to the corner café, LeeAnn ordered her coffee black, and so for the sake of instant camaraderie, I did the same. I longed to fit in.

It was bitter and I worked to conceal the twinge of discomfort creeping to the edges of my mouth as she talked about Asia and described stories beyond the horizon of my imagination. There was a freedom alive within her that I couldn't live another day without.

LeeAnn got up to refill her coffee, and as she did I relinquished the thought that Nova Scotia had been God's test in my faith. My real destiny was Asia.

"You should move to China and work with my kindergarteners."

"I think so, too," I replied instantly as if I'd been waiting for her to ask me this question my entire life.

LeeAnn seemed startled by the ease and certainty of my reaction, but she looked pleased.

I decided over my second cup of black coffee to leave my graduate degree dangling on my fingertips and move as far away from my life in Chico, California, as geographically possible. The destination would be the electric and booming metropolis of Shanghai, China.

God would be there. He'd been there for thousands of years. I would work things out with Him in Shanghai. Nova Scotia would have to wait. My new beginning was East, not north. I would begin again, anew, in Asia.

Long Sweet Pilgrimage

*I will take with me the sun for light
and pearly white moon for romance,
the planet will provide the rest --
lest I offend it by packing.*

    I had three weeks before the shiny airbus would take me across the land covered by the seas. The nights following my decision to leave for Asia were dizzying. I teetered back and forth between my new excitement and old fears.

    I lost hours underneath the oak tree in the backyard dreaming of a life with less anxiety. I tried to contemplate every part of my past, praying that if I did I could leave it all behind.

    I'd spent the past nine months getting in and out of a relationship with a woman who didn't love me, yet provided the outside circumstances I needed to feel rejected. I woke up disliking who I was, and loving Isabel made that easier to deal with.

    She was a few years older than me and unlike any man or woman I'd ever dated. She desperately wanted to be taken care of, but had no desire to reciprocate. Her thoughts were unorganized and her actions could run in direct conflict with themselves, as long as her impulse demanded it.

    With the faint scent of patchouli oil and perpetually wrapped in a scarf, Isabel moved without obligation. No phone call or dinner date or even a question received an answer unless it met her mood or was at the direct mercy of her generosity. In her life, there were no strings, as moving in obligation was somehow a betrayal of the truth.

    Every part of our relationship bore the burden of inequality. I tiptoed around her life, day after day, hoping to be invited back. I knew at a moment's notice she could shift her attention to someone else who could tend to her needs, so I endlessly worked to find new, shiny objects. I craved her rejection.

We rarely made love, and when we did it was unsatisfying. Isabel wanted the pain from her childhood to heal, and I desperately wanted to heal it.

Alas, I couldn't rescue Isabel any more than a raindrop can stop a storm. The only hope there was for a rescue mission was to save myself, and I was too preoccupied trying to save her to figure that out.

In truth, the relationship wasn't entirely fruitless. Unlike my relationship with God, which hinged on guilt and fear, Isabel's story about God was peaceful. I brought Him up as often as I could simply to hear her version.

In Isabel's mind, God was complete and utter love, no matter what words His followers stuffed in His mouth. Life was His gift to us to be celebrated. In that joy, He was honored most. Of course, to her, God wasn't a He at all -- but Everything.

"It just doesn't make sense, Isabel. They talk about an all-loving, all-knowing, omnipotent God, and in the very same breath say He's willing to condemn most of His children to an eternity without Him."

It always came back to fear. It was, after all, the reason I ached. I'd spent the past six years needing Christ most and being denied Him because of the way my heart worked.

When Isabel was in a generous mood, she met my angst about God with reassurance. She explained for the umpteenth time the inherent shortfalls in the human understanding of God's grace.

Isabel had given almost no thought to religion, and didn't speak of it unless I brought it up, which I did, endlessly.

"You've said so yourself, Alexa. In most religious text God demands love and service to others. Yet, the religions that hold those texts to be Truth create a self-obsession around personal salvation. Living a life focused on attaining Heaven and avoiding Hell is the farthest path from what God demanded in those books. God asked us to love Him, and to love one another without judgment."

I listened. It felt harsh but resonated with my experience.

"Religion and God are not the same thing, Alexa. Honestly, how many times do you want to have this conversation?"

I wasn't sure. It felt like the first time. I had decades of data in my brain that linked God to religion, and could hardly fathom a life where those were separated.

"God is love. That's it. Anything short of absolute love is human stuff. Why would God hate you for the way you love? God is love."

I had no idea. I wasn't the one saying God hated gays. Or even worse, that God hated the sin but loved the sinner, as if my love was a sin, as if I could be separated from my sexuality.

"Alexa, if they say God hates the way you love, just imagine what He thinks of the way they judge."

Isabel never expected a comment and I didn't disappointment her by offering one. She wasn't raised thinking she was going to burn in Hell and couldn't fathom the pain I'd endured as a lesbian, fighting for my Father's love. I wasn't just going to give up on Him.

The little satisfaction I got from processing with Isabel gave way to the constant longing I had for something more. I wanted more than she could give and she wanted less than what I was offering.

To my great surprise the idea of moving to China shoved aside any notion I still clung to about rescuing Isabel. I wanted to find my own happiness.

Tugging at my t-shirt, stretching the faces of John, Paul, George and Ringo down my chest, I impatiently waited for Isabel to finish her sentence. I wasn't listening to a word she was saying.

"Are you listening, Alexa?"

"I'm leaving."

Unaffected by my sudden departure, Isabel replied, "Now?"

"I'm moving to China!"

She didn't seem to notice the conversation was about me.

"I've always wanted to travel there. I'll come visit. Send me a ticket when you want company."

Her heart had never been anywhere near mine. "Sure, yeah, okay sure."

It was a thin lie. It was the sort of lie you want to come true but know that it won't. Our entire relationship was a collection of them. I had kept how unsatisfied I was to myself, and so had Isabel.

As my departure date inched closer, I replaced my time spent on God's disapproval with thoughts of adventures on a distant shore.

What use was time spent processing my internal strife with an adventure peeking over the horizon? I could already see the sun rising in the East. It was a deep and delicious orange.

I surrendered my evenings to a Lonely Planet guidebook on China and compilations of traditional Chinese music. I ordered in Chinese food and ate copious amounts of white rice. I needed to practice the fine art of chopsticks. I stopped by the local Asian market to get supplies. This was an adventure, after all.

The little shop smelled like incense soaked in whiskey. I picked up Chinese candles, jasmine tea, incense and a black silk robe with Chinese characters etched across its chest. I imagined it read "Free Yourself," and I wanted to.

When not reading about the Ming, Qing, Tang or Wu dynasties, or about the long-tailed animals on rotisseries to avoid, through the Cliffs Notes my travel guide provided, I reread Henry David Thoreau.

I'd read "Life in the Woods" during high school, but craved the sweet taste of Thoreau's simplicity in my mouth as I prepared my mind to travel East. This was to be my "Life in the Woods"; this was my "Walden". I wanted to leave all my possessions including my fears in search of this new path.

I was to embrace the life Thoreau described when he said the person with the fewest possessions was the freest. I wanted to be free of all things, including my shame and guilt. China would be just that. I was certain that when I got to Asia I could start all over again.

I sold everything I owned to buy a coach seat to cross the mighty ocean. Then I filled seven black garbage bags full of belongings and dropped them off at The Arc thrift store. I cleared the fruity-scented Body Shop lotions and Maybelline make-up that lined the shelves behind my bathroom mirror. Certainly there would be no need for that sort of thing in China -- the land where life had existed since Earth's first sunrise.

As the sun set in the western sky, a pencil-thin, red-headed stewardess walked down the tight airplane aisle. I caught the word Darcy stitched in orange thread on the front of her sweater fighting hopelessly for attention away from her breasts. I tried not to notice how beautiful she was, and asked about a drink instead.

"Yes dear, but you have to wait until we are at our cruising altitude," Darcy offered with a southern drawl buried underneath years of California sunshine.

"Of course, sorry, I'm a bit nervous, that's all. Whenever it's okay I'll take a Jack Daniels on the rocks."

I was terrified of flying, and that dominated my mood. I'd been afraid to fly ever since the moment I learned that God wasn't okay with the way my heart worked. As I waited for my drink to arrive, I tried to distract my nerves by thinking about something other than a plane crash.

I recalled a story I'd heard from a friend in college who told me that once he learned he'd been duped about Santa Claus, all the beliefs he was given as a child were out the window. From that point forward, if a belief emerged in his mind, he decided then and there what to make of it.

This was my then and there. Nothing but newness and uncertainty lie ahead. I had carried the essential items inside my travel pack and wanted to do the same with my mind.

With lukewarm, recycled air circulating around coach, I took out a brown leather journal. I knew myself well enough to know that my adventure would be replaced with fiction if not tediously documented. I was a hopeless, after all. Dreaming about happy endings was how I'd managed to survive with lies and half-truths my entire life.

I needed to write the truth down somewhere. I started my journal with a list, not a poem or a string of prose, just a list of beliefs. I wanted time to grab each one by its roots, shake it off, and examine for the first time if it was something that still resonated with me.

The longer the airbus cut through the skies, the longer my list grew. Most of my beliefs manifested through my black felt tip pen with fear. It didn't surprise me, and I blamed no one in particular for this. This was just the list that emerged. These were the feelings I knew best. These were the feelings I trusted.

I couldn't identify how I'd collected them, but the list was there waiting for me the moment I touched the pen to the paper.

I should be this…
I shouldn't be that…

God only accepts this…
God won't accept that…
If I do this…
If I do that…

As I jotted the beliefs down, I dreamed of life without them. I imagined a life that included God's love and acceptance. I knew Isabel would be proud of me. Then, I reminded myself to let go of the need for her approval, too. It was time to take care of myself.

I imagined a life of simplicity. *How fitting it was to be headed to the East. Oh, yes, I would wake with the sunrise, Tai Chi and contentment.*

I was convinced this ancient land and its ancient ways had more time to understand God. Most importantly, I wanted to believe I could leave my suffering at the departure gate of the San Francisco International Airport.

As the final trace of light faded into the dark Pacific Ocean, I knew without knowing why exactly that my life would never be the same again. I was watering the budding freedom Thoreau had described. At the very least, I was leaving my suffering behind. Or, so I hoped.

Mascara and a Black Cocktail Dress

The very first time the sun rose above the ocean's crust and revealed light upon the earth, inside that moment Asia was born.

Many hours later, the pilot came on the scratchy overhead and announced our final descent. When the announcement in four different languages finally concluded, a joy bubbled up from deep within me.

It had been a much longer trip than I'd expected, but I'd made it. The landing into the Pudong International Airport had begun. *China, oh sweet China, here I come!*

As the wheels hit the tarmac, a symphony of metal clicks emerged. The seat belt sign was still illuminated, but I seemed to be the only one who noticed. The Asian passengers unbuckled their seat belts and stood up.

The airbus slowly taxied across the runway, and as it did my cabin-mates stumbled back and forth in the aisle grabbing their baggage from the overhead bins. *Did they know the statistics on airplane crashes on runways?* I didn't but wasn't taking any chances. I hadn't come all the way to Asia to die during a runway collision. I hadn't made any sort of peace with God yet.

I kept expecting Darcy to race down the aisle tackling people and then politely asking them to get up and sit back down, as she tended to the bruises she caused. But Darcy never arrived. The passengers were free to bump into each other and ignore the seat belt sign altogether.

With everyone up and roaming about, it was suddenly obvious how many people were in such a small space. I felt a tightening of my throat and my armpits dampen.

I suddenly realized my long sweet pilgrimage toward self-acceptance might include more people than I had expected. I couldn't help but imagine God patiently waiting for me in Nova Scotia.

The kindergarten I'd been hired to work for had sent a driver to pick me up from the airport. The man found me as I grabbed my luggage from the airport carousel. His face was a perfect circle and had a gentleness about it that felt familiar. I was grateful for his confident approach, as I would never have picked him out of the crowd.

"Hi Alexa."

"Hi" I replied. I could smell his recent cigarette against my face and moved back slightly. I reached out my hand to greet him.

"It's nice to meet you, ma'am. I'm called Buz."

Buz had a handful of words in English, making my initial minutes in the big city easier than I had expected -- although I hadn't really given much time to imagining what China would look like. The few weeks I had to prepare for my adventure were spent imagining what China would feel like inside of me.

By the time we reached the old minivan in the Shanghai airport garage my nerves tingled with anticipation. I had no idea what the agenda was for the day and questioned why I hadn't asked LeeAnn some of these basic questions in advance of my trip. *Was I really capable of living in China all alone?*

"So Buz, where are we headed?"

"Big. Good. Long. Tour." He offered enough time to each word in English as if it demanded its own sentence.

I tried to meet his enthusiasm with a similar tone.

"Have you ever been to the Great Wall?" I asked.

"Great Wall? No. Shanghai only. Beautiful place -- you will see."

Buz hadn't left Shanghai before and seemed perplexed by my desire for a conversation about something other than what was outside the van window. I noticed my mind fighting to leave Shanghai already and promised to be more mindful.

Even with the muted light casting through the pollution, the silver and gold skyscrapers were sparkling. I'm not certain what I'd expected to see, but it wasn't this. This was the metropolis of all 'metropoli'. This is where 20 million of the 1.3 billion Chinese people reside.

I thought of the items in my suitcase and realized I'd packed for a camping trip on Thoreau's pond, not a huge metropolis. As Buz pointed out fancy restaurants and nightclubs that the tourists enjoyed, I regretted not packing at least one black dress and a tube of mascara.

The city blocks were filled with Starbucks, McDonalds and various other fast food chains from my homeland. Clothing shops and jewelry stores dotted the spaces in between. City cranes occupied more of the skies than the thick brown clouds. People were everywhere.

This is not what communism looked like in my mind. It seemed street vendors were practicing tried and true forms of capitalism. If communism was in Shanghai, it lived in the mother-in-law unit out back.

I tried to shove aside my previous life and its burgeoning problems around my faith, my fight toward self-acceptance and my ongoing negotiations with God about my salvation. I wanted a new start so badly. I had no idea yet that shoving things away gave them more power.

Eventually we pulled into a quiet residential neighborhood. A modest wooden sign signifying the kindergarten flopped against a white picket fence. It looked like rain was coming. I took a huge gulp of air into my lungs and followed him inside.

In order to be accepted into the kindergarten, all children were required to have a foreign passport. An exception was made for children born in Hong Kong because although they were technically Chinese, they were not from the mainland.

Just inside the old front door of the kindergarten, the children were standing in a row. They were ready for a field trip and had been waiting for me to arrive. Buz was also the school bus driver.

So with jet lag still in the corners of my eyes, we piled into a school bus and Buz drove us through the beating heart of Shanghai. Our destination was an indoor playground. Later, I would learn it was an expedition for clean air.

As we cut through the city, I recalled a World Health Organization report I'd found online in preparation for my adventure. It reported that hundreds of thousands of people died each year in China because of pollution. The death toll was equivalent to the entire population of Austin, Texas, dying every year. I kept thinking about the little lungs of the five-year-olds I was crossing the hazy city with. I promised right then to quit having the occasional cigarette.

I ended up across the aisle from Dylan. At three-foot something, Dylan had dark brown hair and even darker eyes. He carried a serious look for a five-year-old and I couldn't help but wonder if life would prove him right or wrong.

Dylan was from Paris and interrupted his native tongue to push around Mandarin or English depending on his audience. He immediately assumed, correctly, that I needed English for the bus ride.

Ling sat beside Dylan. She was a rural Chinese girl but born in Hong Kong and therefore welcomed at the international kindergartens.

Sukanya sat directly beside me with her legs tucked underneath her for a little elevation. She had just arrived from Thailand and kept her head tilted slightly downward by the invisible weight of shyness. I wanted to tell her life got easier with age, but wasn't sure if that was the truth and didn't want to start out with a lie.

Instead, to pass the time as our school bus played chicken with the afternoon vehicles, I engaged the children with conversation.

"Do any of you know what country we live in?" I asked.

The children didn't respond.

So I offered, "You know, like Japan? Or India? Or France?"

Ling quietly responded, "We live in Shanghai, Ms. Alexa."

"You are right, we do live in the city of Shanghai, but does anyone know what country Shanghai is in?"

No one seemed to know, or care, so I shared that Shanghai was in China and was determined to carry on.

"So, which one of you knows where we are headed today?"

Dylan decided this was a boring sequence of questions and offered instead, "Ms. Alexa, people in Japan speak Japanese and in China they speak Chinese."

"Wow, very good Dylan."

I noticed the other students were back to watching our school bus cut through the dense city smog.

"So, Dylan, where do people speak English?"

"Ms. Alexa, everyone knows that -- in Boston!"

I laughed hard, and the children stopped enjoying the traffic and looked at me sideways.

As the others tilted their heads, Sukanya whispered, "Are you okay, Ms. Alexa?"

I knew I wasn't. Anytime I experienced a moment of happiness all the other emotions dwelling inside my heart seemed to come to the surface and rob me of the present moment.

I shook off her question with a question of my own.

"What should we play on first? I heard there is an indoor slide that is as tall as a giant oak tree."

A Guru in Adidas Pants
Just this.

Children are so present. I needed this reminder. If not, I'd easily get caught inside the middle of a hundred worries like back in California before realizing the day was nearly over. I coveted their vigilance to the moment and tried to copy it.

Dylan was quickly becoming my favorite little person to be around. He made poignant observations all of the time, and seemed to have a heightened sense of morality.

If his teacher needed help preparing an activity, Dylan was first to raise his hand. If there was a classroom argument, Dylan often stepped in to neutralize the situation without being prompted or encouraged. He just instinctively responded to conflict with action.

One afternoon at recess, an argument ensued across the yard between two boys over a toy fire engine. As I started to walk over to the boys, I noticed Dylan already in pursuit. He'd noticed the fight, too. He walked up to the boys with a confidence far beyond what his years on earth could justify. I stayed back.

It seemed his abrupt arrival had taken both boys momentarily off guard. Dylan didn't hesitate and instead whispered something into the closer boy's ear. The child immediately dropped the half of the toy engine he was clinging to and ran off toward the swing set.

The other boy in the scuffle was now left standing with the fire engine and Dylan's gentle smile. Instantly uncomfortable with the situation, the child turned and walked away, firmly maintaining his grip on the toy.

Dylan walked over to the sandpit.

"Dylan, what on earth did you say to that boy?"

"What boy?" He seemed to already be lost in his sand castle.

"The boy who took your place in the swing set line."

"Oh, I just told him that recess was almost over and if he went now he could have my turn on the swing."

"But why would you do that? You've been in line for the swing since we got outside."

"Oh, it's no problem for me Ms. Alexa. The problem I have is with fighting. Fighting hurts everyone."

I thought about Martin Luther King, Jr., and Mahatma Gandhi as children and wondered if they sought peace as early as five years old. Maybe I was witnessing the childhood of the next John Lennon.

I looked around at the rest of the class and imagined each of them becoming someone wonderful and happy. I thought of my childhood. It was a good one. It was happy before I realized I wasn't like everyone else.

The children were so trusting, and within days I was met with smiles. They seemed to need help for everything and I loved feeling useful. I started to feel a sense of purpose even amid the uncertainty that living alone in Asia brought.

Most days I all but forgot the work toward self-acceptance I craved when leaving California. I stopped thinking about whether or not God loved me. I was more interested in the folks at the kindergarten and the children liking me.

At the school there was so much to do and such interesting people to fill my minutes with. The office manager was an Australian woman named Amanda who was just a few days older than me, yet had her life already figured out. She had a career and a husband and no doubt a tube of mascara in her bathroom and a black evening gown in her closet.

Amanda and her husband William were easy to like. As if their

Kate Winslet and Hugh Jackman accents weren't attractive enough, they were tall, thin, tan with sky-colored eyes, and sweethearts. The couple worked hard, played hard, and seemed more assimilated to life in the East than some of the Asians I met.

Shanghai was their home and they had the bicycles and a worn-in brown leather sofa to prove it. I lost most minutes with them coveting their lives.

They introduced me to independent films, O'Malley's Pub and what self-confidence looked like. I wanted a love like what I imagined they had, which started with a French press and ended with pillow talk -- a straight person's life.

Many nights after work, I met with LeeAnn, Amanda and William at the Irish pub to sip Guinness and eat potato wedges drowning in sour cream. The waiters zipped around, insuring the bottom of our jugs were never exposed, as my new Australian friends greeted everyone that walked in the massive French oak doors.

O'Malley was an Irish-owned pub in downtown Shanghai that felt nothing like Asia. The only hint of China in the place was the faces pouring the booze. They spoke in perfect English prose with Irish accents, as all hints of Mandarin had been scrubbed clean by the Irish owners.

In a worldly city like Shanghai, this convergence of realities wasn't a surprise, but every time the waiter said, "Another pint, mate?" I grinned and settled into the city life a little more. There was so much about Shanghai I was beginning to love.

Tonight I left the pub early to get a massage. Amanda and William had recently introduced me to the blind massage parlors. These parlors were everywhere, so it wasn't necessary to make an appointment in advance. I just walked to the closest one to the pub and walked in.

I was directed to a table, right away. Unlike the massage I'd grown accustomed to in the United States, in Shanghai, you stay fully clothed and remained so underneath a thin white sheet. I learned that the hard way.

As I was getting my massage I thought of the physical shape I'd been in most of my life. As a collegiate athlete I'd trained, day in and day out, to perform at the highest level I could. It had only been in graduate school that I had started to slack off a bit.

Under the white sheet, fully dressed, I decided it was time to get back into shape. I'd study T'ai Chi Ch'ua. I was living in Shanghai after all.

I beat LeeAnn home by a few hours. When she finally arrived, I asked her about finding a Tai Chi teacher.

She seemed to be in an exceptionally good mood, and excitedly waved her finger in the air with her response. "Oh, Alexa, I know just the guy. Ju--st the peeerfect guy."

Goodbye, Goodbye

God, if you are out there, if you can hear me, please listen to my heart. I'm out of words, today.

The perfect guy was a 22-year-old Tai Chi guru who everyone called Da. My first session was scheduled for the following Monday at the kindergarten right after school ended.

Da rocked black Adidas pants and moved like the wind. He was taller than most of the men I'd seen meandering around the city, standing a good six feet toward the heavens.

Da had a perfectly sculpted and toasted brown body beneath a soft face and meticulously shaved head. He spoke gently and carried a light smile.

There was a depth to him I couldn't understand fully but that pulled at me like the moon pulls at the sun's light. I was mesmerized by his ability to move. He treated gravity like a yo-yo on the end of his finger.

I committed to meeting him every day at the kindergarten playground just after the Chinese nannies picked up their foreign bosses' children. I asked him to teach me what he knew of Tai Chi, but also of the quiet world inside a trained mind.

I spoke of Pema Chödrön and shared my budding interest in the Vietnamese Zen Buddhist, Thích Nhát Hänh. He knew a great deal about him and promised, when the time was right, that all those lessons would be offered.

As you would expect of a Tai Chi master, Da was always on time, looking refreshed and rested. Each night he would greet me with a gentle bow, a soft smile and then walk over to a portable music player and put in a CD filled with sounds of bells and chanting.

"What do you hope to gain from our time together, Alexa?"

I didn't realize I'd be asked such a question and felt ill prepared.

"Um, I'm not sure. I mean, I've been looking for my path for quite some time."

"Path to what?" He replied as if expecting my ambiguity.

"God. I guess."

I knew my answer and had no idea why I was acting as if it was my first day of high school. I was seeking peace with God. I wanted to know if He could love me the way I was.

"Alexa, let me share with you a mistake many people make. They believe there is only one path to God. And before they know it they start to believe that anyone on a different path is lost and in need of saving."

I didn't think I had the only path to God. I didn't have a path at all. But I understood what he was saying. I knew many people that believed their path was the only way to God, as if God had created millions of unique children only to expect them to take the same way home.

"Ok. I will try to avoid that mistake."

"No mistakes we need to learn can be avoided. I simply wanted to acknowledge that paths are like light, they guide us, but depending on where we are coming from and where we are headed, the light may be pointing us in different directions."

So that's where I started -- with Da, day after day, on the artificial grass in the kindergarten's backyard. I couldn't help but imagine what my days would've looked like had I chosen the path of the monastery in Nova Scotia.

The idea of my hours filled with this kind of discipline and devotion seemed to tug at me still. I could still feel the anxiety and fear within me, trying to escape.

"Let's stop here, Alexa."

"I can finish."

"Let us let things be as they are, not as we wish them to be. You are feeling uncomfortable, no?"

"Sad, I guess."

"Let's sit."

We sat down to meditate. Every day Da guided me in mediation before and after our Tai Chi training. I was learning to enjoy the practice most days, but today my mind felt like a mosquito being swatted at by angry hands.

I got up and walked over to the children's swing set. I placed the cold rubber seat underneath me. Da quietly followed.

The moment my hands hit the chains my body fell limp to the ground as if my spine were made of sand. I gasped for air. My ears got warm and very suddenly, my vision blurred.

In an instant, the years of fear about God's disapproval broke through. *How can I be someone other than who I am? Wasn't our love the closest understanding we have of His love? How can I change how I love?*

I'd convinced myself I could deal with a world that disliked me, as long as I had God on my side. But God wasn't on my side. This was the reason for my despair. God's rejection was a burden I could no longer bear alone.

Tiny cold pieces of gravel pressed hard against my cheek, and Da wrapped his arms around me. I let out cries of pain and fear. Tears I'd collected in my heart over the years spilled to the earth. The more tears I cried the more tears emerged.

Da gently whispered over and over again, "'tse.hue, 'tse.hue."

I have no way of knowing how much time elapsed, but at some point I stopped. The moon had crossed the night sky and morning was peeking through. I turned to Da and asked what "'tse.hue" meant.

"It means 'goodbye', Alexa. Those tears represented hurt held in your heart that you are finally ready to let go of. Don't be afraid. Once you let them out they will carry on. They are not your tears any longer. You are ready to heal. This is that beginning."

I knew he was right. The hurt felt like old wounds coming out one tear at a time. The tears were the end of the pain not the beginning. This was a new place.

I desperately wanted to know how Da got me there -- to this place of letting go. I wanted to let all of it out, right now, so that I would never have to feel the pain again. But Da had already taught me that everything has its own time.

With the ache left over after a deep wound has been pried open, and tended to, I walked home. Da insisted on walking beside me. He didn't say another word, nor did I. There was nothing to say. He walked me to my door, bowed his head slightly and then walked away.

My body yearned to grab for him and ask him to stay. I wanted him to know all of the pain still left inside of me so he could help heal it. But that healing was my job. No one, not even Da, could resolve this struggle.

I didn't know what time it was and didn't feel the least bit hungry. Instead I laid on the couch and started to let sleep in. As I did, I realized that everything I'd been running from in America had boarded the airbus with me.

I knew dealing with my pain was why I'd crossed the seas in the first place, but now that I was here, and the hurt was exposed, I just wanted to hide.

¿Como Sé Dice?

It was misting outside when I woke up. I wasn't ready for things to be fully illuminated yet and welcomed it. I thought of the little drops of moisture trapping all that air pollution and sprinkling it on to the earth below.

I'd been sleeping on LeeAnn's couch for months now. On the coffee table beside me was a stack of Mandarin study cards I'd made before I left Chico. They were tattered and coffee-stained but of great importance to me nevertheless. I flipped through them.

Door, *hu*.

Kitchen, *chu*.

Morning tea, *zaocha*.

Knowing some basic words in Mandarin made me feel better even though the language was more difficult than I'd expected. I hadn't really considered the change in alphabets.

Unlike the Spanish I studied during high school, Mandarin seemed to awaken parts of my brain not yet functioning. I couldn't just sound out words like I would street signs in Mexico.

To add complexity to the already difficult task of learning a new language, the benefits of immersion were irrelevant here, as very few people around me spoke Mandarin.

Shanghainese was most common on the streets, with a mix of other languages tossed in by roaming expatriates. Still, I was bent on studying, so after my tea, I called Da and asked if he knew anyone who might be my language teacher.

"You feeling okay, Alexa?"

"Yeah. I think so. Sort of feel like I have the flu or something."

"Yes, I left a bag of tea at your door. Please prepare it as my note describes. You will feel better afterward. It's not the flu. It's healing."

This morning it felt like anger but I didn't want to disappoint my new friend. I was surprised to hear that he had already been by LeeAnn's place.

As Da explained the importance of sitting with unsettled feelings, I walked to the door and found a small brown bag sitting on the doormat.

"I'd like to study Mandarin. Do you know a teacher?"

"Did you find the tea, sister?" he offered, avoiding my question.

"I did. Thank you."

"Drink the tea. Don't trouble your mind now with new distractions. Just take time to sit with last night. Drink the tea as often as you need today. Only leave the house to walk a bit with your thoughts, if you feel you need to move."

Of course, I needed to move. "I need to go to work, Da."

"Today is Saturday. Just rest."

I hung up the phone and made the tea. I felt a sense of fear sneak in which offered evidence in my mind -- to my mind -- that I was too weak to heal these wounds alone. *How could I be expected to find peace with God and my sexuality when I didn't even know the day of the week?*

I didn't move off of the couch for hours. LeeAnn was in Hong Kong with Amanda and William for the weekend so I was there alone. I had the television on but muted. I wanted to feel less lonely and the light emanating through the screen created that illusion.

It struck me as I was watching unfamiliar faces on the television reveal expressions of happiness and joy, that I was missing out on the lighter side of life.

Today, I felt like blaming God. I was tired of blaming myself and I felt angry that He'd made me this way -- only to abandon me. So instead of praying, I just talked to myself. I didn't care if God listened or not. I'd been fighting to hold on to Him my entire life and it had only caused me pain.

If God didn't love me as I was, there was nothing I could do about it. I'd spent my entire life trying to be someone other than who I was and hadn't succeeded. I needed to let Him go for now and deal with my eternity when the time came. *That was it. It was time to let go of God.*

I was shocked to realize that the thought brought immediate relief. *Why hadn't I thought of this before?*

I didn't know yet that at the edge of real healing the mind begs us to retreat to the familiar, even if that guarantees more pain. I said it again, and this time, out loud... *it's time to let go! I mean it. Let go, Alexa. If you ever want to feel better you need to move on.*

I couldn't bear putting God's name in the sentence but we both knew who I was talking about.

I got up to make something to eat. Boiled eggs and tea had become my staple since I arrived, so I boiled water for both, then ate enough until my stomach was full.

By nightfall I felt better. I was hoping with a little sleep I'd be up for tending to the rowdy five-year-olds by Monday morning. Just as I started to doze off, the phone rang and startled me. *It's so late for a call. It must be someone from home.* I immediately questioned my decision to let go of God. *What if something was wrong and I needed Him?*

As it turned out Da had heard my plea for help in finding a language teacher and Ginger's call was his response. She was obviously a night owl.

During the call, Ginger invited me to meet her at a local pizzeria every day, except Sundays, to learn and practice Mandarin. It was a big commitment to make half asleep but I made it anyway. I was relieved; I hadn't needed God for this news after all.

She told me we'd start tomorrow, even though it was a Sunday, and then hung up without waiting for an answer. It wasn't rude, I knew now, it was just China.

The pizzeria had red leather booths and checkered tablecloths underneath glass tabletops. There was an old Arcade game leaning against the back wall although its screen seemed shadowy and untouched for years.

Black and white photos of Hollywood celebrities donned the walls and if no one spoke a word I could've tricked myself into believing I was in the Big Apple.

I slid into the booth where a young woman was waving me toward her.

"Hi."

"Ni Hao."

I repeated it as best I could, understanding the importance of a first impression.

She didn't seem impressed.

"Please teach me to read and write, not just memorize sounds, Ginger."

Ginger didn't laugh because Chinese folks don't laugh directly at your face when you say something ridiculous, but I felt like she wanted to.

Instead she gracefully brushed her shoulder-length, straight black hair from on her shoulders to behind them, and proceeded to explain the differences in our languages.

"A-wreck-sa, it's A-wreck-sa, right?"

"Yes." It was her best, I could tell, so there was no reason to say it my way. I also wanted to set a precedent of appreciating effort. I knew I'd be in need of it.

"Your language was created for your ears. Our language was created for our eyes. You will not learn to read and write without proper schooling. But if we practice talking together every day, one day soon, you will know the words being used many lifetimes before your language was born."

I had an open laboratory for practice so I tried not to squander it by being intimidated. I rode public transportation almost daily now and used it as a chance to start a dialogue with anyone who looked me in the eyes, which was few and far between. Still, I tried.

Often times on the Shanghai Metro when I'd finally engage a conversation-mate, out of the deep crevices of my mind, "Como se dice?" would emerge, uninvited and unwelcomed.

It was humbling but this was my self-proclaimed new beginning. I had dreamed of this new life during my darkest moments back home, and if it saddled up with a little humility then so be it.

A Piglet Named Parkson

I'd been crashing at LeeAnn's house for months now to ease the blow that Asia strikes into a sheltered Westerner's gut. LeeAnn was assimilated to life in China and it made my transition somewhat bearable.

She was kind and generous and seemed to have a similar need for cohabitation. A huge part of me wanted to try living alone, but moving to China made breaking down my unhealthy habits less urgent.

LeeAnn also had boatloads of pirated DVDs, knew how to order in Italian food, and could easily get from one side of Shanghai to another. So I was less motivated than I should've been to test my wings. Our friendship was effortless at first and I didn't mind the familiarity of being around an American.

"Let's go to the shopping district after work, Lex."

I was desperate to practice my Mandarin with strangers, also curious where the label "Paris of East" came from, so I jumped on the offer. I also needed mascara.

As it turned out, I was the only woman at the kindergarten without makeup on. In fact, I felt like the only foreigner in Shanghai without makeup on. The fact that I'd packed for a camping trip was not working out.

A few minutes after the last child was picked up from the school a blue taxicab pulled in front of the kindergarten. Most of the cabbies were friendly and this guy was no exception. He turned around with a smile to greet us.

LeeAnn looked at me as if inviting me to practice my new Mandarin, but I wasn't ready to practice when money was on the line. I shook off her offer.

Downtown Shanghai reminded me of Chicago. There were no significant similarities, other than the typical big city stuff, but after years of rural life, places with skyscrapers looked alike. The sticky air reminded me of how many people were breathing beside me, and the piercing sounds of car horns and sirens interrupted the constant hum of conversation.

I shut my eyes for a moment and imagined the sweet scent of street-roasted chestnuts in the zippy crisp Chicago air. My heart jumped back to a memory tucked deep inside my mind.

I was nine years old. My parents were still together. We lived against a cornfield in Valparaiso, Indiana, a place where it was safe to play in the streets day or night and lightning bugs provided as much entertainment as needed.

It was a short chapter of my life but it remained unharmed and protected by adolescent memories sandwiched between the tooth fairy and Santa Claus. In those memories school days were occasionally snowed out and Cabbage Patch Dolls were all that was needed for happiness.

On this winter day, my mom hustled around the house getting us ready for a family trip. She was always capable of completing three tasks at once. The afternoon was mild so she and my father had decided to take us to see the live performance of Nutcracker in Chicago.

My older brother, twin sister and I were as excited about the family time as we were about a trip to the city. In the backseat of the family station wagon we fought our strongest instincts to misbehave. I sat between my siblings because I seemed to irritate Tharyn just slightly less than Alisha did.

I had hoped that would remain true tonight, as we'd been talking about getting the street roasted chestnuts and I didn't want anything to spoil our adventure in Chicago.

Dad drove as mom worked to entertain us with games that could be played without our hands. Games including hands always ended in tears. As we crossed the state line into Illinois the dense city lights looked like our little town's evening sky had been turned upside down. The buildings sparkled. I'd never seen so many flickers of white so close to the earth before.

Shanghai's reminder of Chicago sent a wave of homesickness over me. Fortunately LeeAnn interrupted my angst with a tug for help with the massive department store door. As we collectively pressed it open, a loud squeak came from beside the entrance.

Had we hit something? We stopped pushing and turned our heads toward the direction of the sound. As we did, a short, round man emerged from a shadowy spot against the department store wall.

"Ni Hao."

"Ni Hao." LeeAnn responded.

I was late to respond but I knew what to say, so I did, stepping forward, "Ni. Ni Hao."

By now the man had shoved a cardboard box into view by kicking it forward with his foot, and four pairs of malty brown eyes looked up at us.

The first three I noticed had the unmistakable look of puppy dogs. The fourth, however, refused to fight for the top of the pile and instead pushed to the side of the box and into our view. *A plea for help?*

LeeAnn and I were left without options. She haggled with the man for a few minutes, then we wrapped *Parkson* up and took him home. We never made it into the department store and I promised myself I'd borrow mascara from Amanda first thing tomorrow.

In retrospect, perhaps, we should've taken a minute to consider the amount of work a little piglet would be. But his life was on the line and there had been no real time available to properly analyze the situation.

If I had truly considered the fate of the puppies they would have returned home in our taxicab, too. But, I hadn't and they hadn't. In my Western mind the baby pig had been the only one in imminent danger of an early death.

Parkson had to be bottle fed for a couple weeks, although it was obvious what he really needed was his mother's nipple and a dirty pigsty to sleep in based on how unsettled he seemed.

LeeAnn took all of the middle-of-the-night shifts and never complained. Parkson was safe from the rotisserie, and his constant need for love and attention helped my heart feel more attached to China.

After weeks of the bottle and with a little blanket of fat around his edges, Parkson was finally ready to live underneath the sun and the moon.

LeeAnn had Buz build him a permanent home at the kindergarten. The children instantly adored him and he them. With a place of his own Parkson grew at an astronomical rate. I took it as a sign I needed to get my own place too. I was perpetually looking for signs. It was something I'd done since I was a child. I'd always wanted to know if God was out there and trying to talk to me.

LeeAnn had been a tremendous help but I found myself depending on her for things I needed to learn on my own. I also felt her wanting things from me I'd never be able to offer.

Sweet Stench of Fried Fish

*Your heart holds the only mirror with your true reflection.
Look there.*

Da's voice was always soothing.

"I hope I can help, Alexa. Let's meet at KFC on XianXia Road. Would this be suitable for you?"

"Oh KFC, yes KFC, great, one of my favorites," I replied with a gentle lie, the kind of lie you wedge in the door for kindness to walk through.

I hung up the phone and walked over to the kitchen table. Underneath it were little straw remnants from Parkson's time with us.

I pulled out my journal and wrote down a few of the repeating thoughts floating around in my mind. I knew the best hope I had for letting them go was to write them down. If not I'd recycle them all afternoon. Da was encouraging me to let things keep moving.

I sat for a few minutes paying attention to my thoughts like he'd instructed. I'd thought about God even more since I decided to let Him go.

I walked over to the sink and filled a glass with tap water and took a huge gulp. It tasted like rotten air so I spit it out. Then I called LeeAnn to ask whether the tap water was okay to drink.

This was another one of those questions I wondered how I'd managed to avoid asking. I'd already been in China for three months. *Had I not had a single glass of water yet?*

"Is the tap water safe to drink?"

LeeAnn laughed hard. "Of course, not. What's gotten into you?

You know you can't drink the water here."

It sounded right so I carried on. "I'm supposed to meet Da for KFC in a little bit. Would you mind giving me a lift?"

"Sure. I'll be home soon."

I decided if my search for a new place went well with Da then I would tell LeeAnn I was moving out. I'd wait until after I found a new place. I was learning she was like a wine glass on carpet -- easily upset.

By the time I got to the fast food joint I'd spent my days in America avoiding, I was actually quite hungry. The menu looked like it had been modified slightly as I couldn't imagine American folks in the Midwest ordering grass jelly milk tea.

From the looks of it Da had been there awhile and was already halfway through a box of extra-crispy chicken. On the back of a paper placemat he was sketching out Shanghai. His attention to detail was unbelievable.

Everything Da did, he did with such intention. The way he washed his hands. The way he made tea or instructed me in Tai Chi. This was certainly mindfulness. There was a sense of calm about him that I yearned for.

Da had laid out the sections of the city -- Pudong, Bund, French Concession, Putuo, Yangpu and HongQiao -- and, what appeared to be a plan to visit certain areas in a search for my new home.

After we ate, Da, patiently and meticulously, drove us around the busy city streets. As he drove I tried to soak up landmarks I might remember later. But after a short while the city seemed to blend together.

The dark gray apartment buildings were all at least ten stories high. It didn't seem to matter what time of day we arrived, the hallways were emanating smells of fish and spices.

The balconies dripped of clothing that seemed to transcend the centuries because the Chinese never adopted dryers. The elevators were rickety. The hallways were teeming with women in silk pajamas and the common area carpet unscathed by tenants was filled with children's toys. It didn't feel like home. Well, it didn't feel like my home; it felt like a million other people's.

By our last stop I decided I wanted LeeAnn's couch and a hot shower more than room to grow.

Old French Concession

*We so often rush
only to find
when we get there
we're not ready.*

Then straight out of the hazy skies, on the very next Tuesday, right after snack time, as the children curled up for their naps, Amanda received a call at the front office. It was a woman who'd heard there was an American looking for a place to rent. That's how fast information traveled in this ancient city, something that baffled me as millions lived here.

As it turned out a young Shanghainese woman named Qin was preparing to move to the United States to start law school but was helping her parents move into the rental business first. The Chen family owned a little place in the French Concession District.

My condo was one of dozens in a locals-occupied part of the District. I had the corner unit so my little flat absorbed all the sights, sounds and smells of the street peddlers.

The first sunrise in my new place, a man arrived outside of my window at precisely 5 o'clock in the morning. I knew what time it was because I was already awake and staring at the Gucci watch I'd picked from a street vendor. I was glad to see it was working since it only cost me $3 US dollars.

The man was on a bike that like his face wore the undiscriminating consequences of gravity. He had tattered baskets tied to his bike's rickety behind. Inside the woven baskets were dozens of fussy chickens stacked on top of each other.

As the peddler settled in underneath my living room windowsill he began ringing a silver bell. How that tiny object projected that magnitude of sound was astonishing to me.

I'd gotten up a few minutes before sunrise and started to boil water in my tea kettle. I found the cold mornings in Shanghai more bearable with hot tea and it made me feel more connected to Asia than brewing coffee.

When the tea kettle started to sing the peddler began announcing his daily product line. It was an enthusiastic announcement of the size and price of each little feathered creature behind him or so I imagined. I couldn't understand a word.

As I sipped on the leaf-flavored water I watched my neighbors' front doors fly open and women of all ages sprint toward the bell. These same women could be found lingering in their silk pajamas as the sun followed its elliptical path with no sense of urgency to meet the day.

The first woman to the bike pointed to her chicken of choice. It was a smaller hen than the others and for a brief moment I imagined her bringing home a pet -- a pet chicken. I was still new to China and my thoughts were proof of it.

The old peddler wrapped his aged hands around the feet of the unlucky chicken lingering at the end of her fingertip, and then quickly ended my naïveté with the snap of the little feathered life.

That was the first and last time I looked outside of my window at 5 a.m.

Even though I started to anticipate things like the chicken man's morning bell and the smells emanating from my neighbors' windows at dawn, I still wasn't sure if I was adjusting to life in Asia. Honestly, I didn't know what adjustment would feel like but I assumed it would feel like something other than this.

The expats I worked with talked about an "in-between time". That is to say, the time that existed in between being here and being there (wherever you'd been before here).

Even with their reassurance, I felt like a hibernating bear waiting for spring. I was waiting to feel content; waiting to feel happiness;

waiting to feel better -- perpetually waiting. It was a familiar feeling as I brought it with me from California.

As a distraction during my in-between time, I worked to emulate the well-traveled urban expat lifestyle I was surrounded by. I desperately wanted to fit in -- even with the progress I was making with Da. I'd grown used to compartmentalizing my life and it wasn't difficult to carry on that way in China.

With Da I worked to open up and heal. I wanted to know the truth and make room it. I wanted to accept who I was. But when I wasn't with Da I seemed to slip into old habits, longing for other people's acceptance and approval.

I filled my flat in the old French Concession District with IKEA couches and lamps. Since, I was the only foreigner within a five mile radius, I stuck out no matter what -- why not have the orange IKEA couch and cloth lamp shades too?

All the clothes left in California during my brief "Thoreau-ian moments" were replaced with city threads from the boutiques that lined the streets of Shanghai.

Almost a month had passed in my new digs and I knew the best place to buy meat on a stick, boiled eggs and French baguettes. These were things no one else had taught me, things I had discovered all on my own. I could greet the vendors in their native tongue with "tzoh'eu" and offer an abundance of Shanghainese "please and thankyous."

When I got back home from school I slipped off my street shoes and on my thin black house shoes resting by the front door. I burned incense and played music I'd borrowed from Da. I was adjusting a little.

I rarely made phone calls home because somehow being alone with all this uncertainty seemed more manageable. But today with the new realization that I was adjusting a little to life in Asia, I felt like sharing it with someone. I suppose I still felt like a sunrise was more beautiful if I could share it.

"Hi Isabel!"

"Oh, Lex. Hi! How are you?"

"I'm doing alright. It's so different here. Just yesterday I noticed that people..."

Isabel interrupted, "Oh I was just on my way to Bidwell Park for a walk, maybe I can call you later tonight?"

Had she forgotten I was in China? I was calling from China. I was making my one call and it was to her. I could've easily called someone who would have been excited to hear from me but I chose Isabel. These were the sorts of decisions I was trying to change by moving across the Pacific but I obviously still needed more time to learn.

I offered something about missing her and then hung up. I felt like telling her how insensitive she was and that I'd wasted my happy new feeling of adjusting in Asia on her but there was only one person to tell that to and it wasn't her.

"Thanks Lex. Talk to you later then."

I still wanted to talk to someone. So even after she hung up I held the cell phone against my ear. Unlike a landline there was no dial tone, just empty air, so I carried on as if she was still there.

"You know Isabel, I let go of God."

In my mind, Isabel responded with a gentle misleading tone -- the sort that sneaks in with judgment before you notice it.

"Alexa, when are you going to understand that God's existence, just like God's love, has nothing to do with what you do or don't do, or think or don't think. It just is."

I had to admit she made a good point and I was tempted to reconsider my earlier plan to let Him go, if that was the case.

Could my thoughts have no impact on what was or wasn't? If that was true, then maybe my thoughts, and everyone else's thoughts, about God's disapproval of who I was were also irrelevant.

Eventually I put the phone down. I thought about the moment right before someone goes insane. There must be a split second before the thin line between sanity and insanity is crossed. *Was this that moment -- that line?*

I'd always worried about losing my mind. It was a senseless yet real worry. I hit the 'end' button on my phone three times to make sure God understood that I knew no one was there. I had known it all along. I was just lonely. *Couldn't He understand me, just once?*

Of course, I still believed in God, in my mind. That hadn't gone away with my recent fight to let Him go from my heart. I was just exhausted and wanted to worry about something else for once.

I walked to the bathroom and washed my hands. The hand washing had taken the place of lighting a cigarette. I was washing my hands ten to twenty times a day now. I knew what this would sound like if I told anyone, so I kept it to myself. I justified it with an explanation that I missed the water. I needed water. Shanghai's dirty river was not helping things. *Where was the ocean I'd imagined?*

Regardless of my neurotic behavior, I knew losing my mind was not an option. *I will not lose my mind. I will not lose my mind. I will not. Will not. You hear me? You can take anything but that. Are you listening?*

I opened the fridge and grabbed the leftover meat skewers I'd picked up the day before from a street vender. It was cold chewy meat at this point and didn't taste very good.

Almost instantly my stomach felt unsettled. It was impossible to know if it was from my phone call, the self-talk, or the meat. They were all likely culprits. I'd forgotten why I started eating meat again and temporarily swore it off.

An evening walk seemed like a good way to clear my head and let my stomach digest. Da always said, if tea doesn't work then walk.

There was a newly renovated café with black and white tiled floors, contemporary lights dripping from the ceiling, which I passed on my walk home from work each evening.

It was located in the shopping part of the District on the same block as the pizzeria. I put on the Asia garment Da had given me for Tai Chi in hopes of feeling calm. I locked up the house and walked the mile or so to the café.

When I walked in Yanni was playing through the overhead speakers. The place felt more like a night club than a café and I felt underdressed. I pulled out a stool at the bar and sat down.

To my great surprise I found Macallan sitting on the top shelf, my favorite single malt scotch. When I pointed to it to place my order, the bartender grabbed the Macallan 18. *Didn't he know it was too smoky and would lure me outside to have a cigarette?*

I'd quit after my first bus ride with the children and had no interest in tempting my strength. I wanted the Macallan 12 -- on the rocks. I was tired of thinking.

One glass of single malt led to another and in no time the moon was looking down from the highest point in the sky. It was late. It had to be close to midnight so I left for home.

When I rounded the corner to my block all the lights were out. The street was charcoal gray and if I hadn't been in a Chinese city I might have been frightened. Fortunately I caught my kitchen light spilling into the alleyway. I was glad to see I'd forgotten to shut it off.

As I got closer to the condo, I heard familiar voices coming from my flat. I thought it was odd but just a few hours ago I'd had a conversation with someone who wasn't actually on the phone any longer. *How much had I had to drink anyway?*

As I peeked through the living room window I saw Mr. Chen, my landlord, lying with his feet up on my IKEA couch. He wore black house slippers and a robe. I stood outside rummaging through the dim lighting to collect my thoughts before I walked in.

Somehow he knew I was out for the evening and apparently had decided to stop in, and while there, watch the bootlegged movie I'd started the night before. It was Meg Ryan's voice I had recognized from the street.

I gave him an awkward look from the entrance way as I took off my shoes. Mr. Chen grabbed the side of the couch for help to get up and without a suggestion of embarrassment slowly let himself out.

"Ni hao, Qin."

"Ni hao, ma. Everything ok?" Mr. Chen's daughter responded a bit startled by the late call.

"Well, yes, mostly, but I wanted to ask you a favor."

"Sure, what is it Alexa? Do you want to go shopping tomorrow, or do you need to know the name of a good doctor?"

I hesitated for longer than appropriate. *A good doctor?*

"Actually, no. You see I just got home and your dad was sitting on my couch watching a movie. And, well, it's midnight."

"Oh, I'm sorry. Things are very different here than what you are used…"

I interrupted her with, "I realized that when I noticed he was eating my leftovers out of the fridge."

I was grateful I called Qin. Most of my life I would've been more concerned about making sure Mr. Chen and Qin liked me than to take care of my own needs. I took it as a measure of progress and crawled in bed.

Little Worn and Wooden Toothpick

He held out a white porcelain bowl to offer the last bit of rice to a stranger. Stranger to him would have been to offer nothing at all.

The following day I came home from the kindergarten and was pleased that my landlord was nowhere in sight; however, perched on my doorstep like three little birds were my next-door neighbors.

In harmony they stood up. Their daughter lifted up her hand as if carrying a bowl of rice beside her cheek and then proceeded to shovel imaginary rice into her mouth. The movements were unmistakable. This was a dinner invitation.

Mr. Huang cooked in the kitchen while I sat in the living room with his 'one child' and her mother. As has been written in nearly every book during the 21st century that mentions the words 'China' and 'child' it is no secret that the creatively conceived policy of 'one child' for the urban folk and 'two children' for the rural people had created a debacle of great proportions.

I overheard two men discuss in a coffee house, most recently, that China would go to war within the decade in order to preoccupy the men that will never have wives or families of their own, not even girlfriends to distract them. There were simply not enough females being made to match up with the males and that meant trouble.

The grey haired gentleman with blue jeans and a worn tweed jacket argued that the only possible way to kill off a generation of men, who will inevitably end up making trouble, was to send them to war.

It seemed a ludicrous argument to me and to the young man he was trying to convince but I could hardly come up with an alternative scenario. I decided that ten years was surely enough time for a plan to be developed and went back to my espresso.

Now inside my neighbor's house I was hoping to be offered a cup of tea to distract from the instant sensation of claustrophobia. Although our condos were right next to each other theirs was a quarter mine's size.

Mr. and Mrs. Huang shared their small condo with their 16-year-old daughter. There was a living room, a bathroom and a kitchen, no bigger than the size of a one-car garage in the US. I imagined all the teenagers I knew back at home and what they might think of this arrangement.

The kitchen table folded up into one wall so that a Murphy bed could fall out of another. They had things stuffed and tucked and shoved in every crevice.

The television was tucked into our shared wall and there were two posters directly across from it. David Beckham filled the edges of one and a young Pamela Anderson in Baywatch donned the second.

I glanced up at them once, then a second time, and then all of a sudden realized this whole thing might be a dream. It was the poster of Pamela Anderson that got me thinking I might still be sound asleep in my bed in Chico, with Billie Holiday still spinning around my record player, and the monastery admittance forms clutched in my fist.

I'd memorized the all-important phrase, *"Duì bù qǐ, cèsuǒ zài nǎr?"* which literally meant, "Excuse me, bathroom be where?"

Mrs. Huang pointed me down a short hallway.

I rinsed my face for a few minutes. I needed the water. In the pocket sized mirror, nailed above the sink, I looked at my reflection. *Was I dreaming?*

I couldn't tell. I splashed more water on my face and then dabbed it dry with the only towel hanging in the bathroom. I pictured all three of them using it. It smelled funny and I clenched my teeth to avoid gagging.

By the time I walked back into the main room preparations for dinner were underway. To my surprise, it was Mr. Huang not Mrs. Huang who set the table.

When dinner was ready Mr. Huang walked out from the kitchen

and placed a huge iron pot onto the little wooden table. I was newly ex-vegetarian and the first thing that caught my eye was a fish head bobbing up and down like a buoy.

I'd just had a bad experience with meat skewers and had sworn off meat again, but realized another exception would have to be made. I was at my neighbor's house in Shanghai. Next to the soup there were tiny snail shells spread across a baking sheet.

It only took being in China for seconds, to realize that everything and anything that was once moving, even slightly crawling, was fair game for cuisine. Chocolate was no longer a necessity for things with miniature wings and legs. Insects were sold and as is -- no milk, dark, or sea-salt variety needed.

Mr. Huang handed me a snail. He looked down at my hand and then with a slight nod of his head upward, he nudged me to eat it. I froze with uncertainty. *Do I suck it? Pick it out? Eat the crunchy shell too?* There must be the way to get the little snail hiding inside out. I hoped it was dead. I paused again.

The second pause proved helpful as Mr. Huang seized the opportunity to show me by example. He grabbed a toothpick from his shirt pocket and stabbed inside the shell. A slimy teriyaki marinated snail emerged into the light. He placed it into his mouth and let out a universal sound of satisfaction.

Then Mr. Huang handed me his little, worn and wooden toothpick. I wasn't sure which took more courage -- eating the slightly cooked snail or using the toothpick that had no doubt taken up permanent residency in my neighbor's shirt pocket.

China was challenging everything I knew about hygiene and personal space. With so many people around me, nothing was solely my own anymore. Not my seat on a bus or a train, not my space in a line, everything was interrupted by another person's presence. I knew there were lessons I needed to learn here but the list seemed to be getting longer by the minute.

Monks and the Lotus Flower

*Sweet Darling,
your heart is the sun
your mind -- the moon
for there is only one light
the other but a reflection.*

After work, Tai Chi and Mandarin lessons each evening I gave myself a few hours to wander around the wrinkled city. Shanghai held secrets collected over the centuries, I was convinced, and wanted to discover them.

I went back to devouring street food and stumbled around the beautiful temples and quiet bookstores unmolested by tourists.

I grabbed the shallow quest for adventure I still had and fought the instinct to head back to the French Concession every time I found something challenging. During the process I even started to enjoy myself.

Today, I had gotten a late start to my wandering about. Ginger had been tardy to our session because her mother had an accident of some sort. She didn't offer any more information and I was learning not to ask questions that felt personal.

As the sky started to spit a little I caught a massive temple out of the corner of my eye. I'd made it to the western side of the giant city's face without noticing how late it was. The temple had already closed for the day.

I found my way back to the Jade Buddha Temple the following day. The lotus flowers engraved on the stone floor captured the essence of the place. The temple overflowed with local worshipers. Monks quietly walked around in meditation and I sensed contentment in the air. This was the feeling I'd been craving from my room in Hill's house in Chico.

This was what I had imagined Asia would hold. Everything in me wanted to ask how I could sign up, don an orange robe, and send a postcard to the kindergarten and to home, notifying everyone who cared, that God had called -- it really was Him this time.

I'd only been in China a little more than five months but my longing for the monastic lifestyle was still alive inside of me. That I couldn't deny. Although my time with the children was precious, I was still pulled to the idea of becoming a nun.

With a desperate need for insight I called Da.

"You alright?" He asked with the gentle sound of someone quiet on the inside.

"Are we still on for later this evening?"

"Yeah, I'm okay. I'm good actually. I found the Jade Buddha Temple and didn't want to leave. I haven't told you this but I think I'm meant to be a nun. Before I left for China I was planning to move to Nova Scotia to train and live under the spiritual training of Pema Chödrön. After all this time in Shanghai the only peace I've felt was at the temple today. "

"You're ready, sis."

"Ready? Ready for what?"

"Your journey here is unfolding in its own perfect time. You are ready to take another step." Da carried on, "Go home and rest. I'll see you at the kindergarten at blue.

I did as he said. Then slightly before dusk when the sky was as blue as it gets in Shanghai I put on Adidas pants and hailed a cab to the school. Da greeted me at the door and handed me a large red book. It was the Tibetan Book of Living and Dying.

Maybe Da had already seen through me. Perhaps, he knew my greatest fear was dying before God and I had made peace. In my mind, until God came down and told me He loved me as I was, a part of me believed my eternity contained fire and brimstone. The only resolution I'd ever come up with was dedicating my life to Him completely. *If I denied all earthly desires would He still punish me for my unused sexuality?*

This had been my race to and from Christ my entire life. Perhaps,

Da knew all of this already. I'd sensed a deep knowing just under his words. Maybe Da understood that just holding a book with a title which included the word "dying" caused a chill down my spine. *Was I inviting the angel of death to my doorstep if I said the word aloud?* I wasn't ready to die. I knew that.

But even with my fear of death I was beginning to trust Da with my broken pieces. I'd seen glimpses of light in our work together.

So I accepted the massive red book and prayed that evening to the angel of death for a bit more time to sort things out. I wasn't ready to die yet. I didn't know if God would take me this way and so -- *I needed more time, please.*

I went to the temple as often as possible. I found my way to tranquil little gardens and quiet places the tourists didn't discover during their two-hour tour. I read the words of Sogyal Rinpoche and as best I could I carved out space for his wisdom to rest inside my heart.

I drank tea and talked to God. I realized early on that the way of praying I had been taught -- to share, to ask, to wish, to offer gratitude -- was no longer comforting me. If God was at the temple I wanted to hear Him. If nothing else I wanted to learn to quiet my mind to improve my chances.

The Temple was the perfect backdrop for meditation. It had been around since 1882 when it was constructed to house two jade Buddha statues. A monk brought them to Shanghai from Burma and had crossed the seas with these white jade statues. Not even the revolution that had overthrown the Qing Dynasty had hurt the statues. The temple around the statues had fallen to ruins yet, the Sitting Buddha and Recumbent Buddha remained unharmed.

This inspired me. It gave hope to the crumbled pieces held together inside of my chest. I made my way to these statues on each visit to the temple.

I listened to the constant murmuring of tourists walking by. I loved this new way of connecting with God by just focusing on my breath. I was so grateful for all of Da's training at the kindergarten. I used his lessons as I sat inside the sacred walls.

At the temple I felt quiet, not an overwhelming silence, just glimpses of quiet from time to time. God appeared to be quiet too but at least if He tried to talk to me I wouldn't be interrupting.

When I wasn't at the temple I was longing to be there. Although the children at the kindergarten filled me with joy, my personal quest could no longer be contained by fleeting happiness. I felt things changing.

After I'd moved to the French Concession my relationship with LeeAnn changed too. Of course, it had to. We had both grown accustomed to an unsustainable act; the routine where I needed her to survive in China and she needed me to need her, to survive. That wasn't possible with our new arrangement. I hadn't really liked it to begin with.

I still needed the gig at the kindergarten but decided if I lost the job because our friendship was changing then so be it. I need to be alone. *If not, how would I ever find a way to like myself?*

Field of Blue Poppies

In the quiet we can finally hear.

Winter arrived the following morning. I wasn't sure if all the seasons came unannounced in the middle of the night but it seemed winter had. Even with big jackets purchased for cheap at the Xiaong Market the cold made wandering around the city more difficult than during the hazy fall days.

If I couldn't spend my evenings wandering around the city I really needed to get to a gym and work out. Exercise had always helped me manage my mind. One of the teachers at the kindergarten suggested Gold's Gym. It sat directly across the city from where I lived. Although I'd never gone to this privately owned gym in the United States, in China anything from home seems comforting, so I joined.

I imagined other foreigners would be there on their journey toward self. I couldn't be the only one who moved to Asia to find myself.

Actually it was Da's idea that I join the gym and I was beginning to trust his instincts. He knew my level of anxiety and thought a good daily sweat couldn't hurt. He was right and I knew it. I promised him I'd work out on Tuesdays and Thursdays.

He promised me that if I increased my strength and endurance through a gym workout, he would add a martial arts component to my daily Tai Chi and meditation. That was all the incentive I needed. I craved externally imposed discipline. It was what I'd grown accustomed to as a collegiate athlete. It was still a crutch.

In China I often imagined my life was unfolding like a movie. Everything was so different than my life before. The martial art training was the part of the film toward the middle when the music started to play. The martial art scenes depicted the positive turn in the protagonist's life. This was when things started to get better and lead the story toward the happy-ending.

I would work out at Gold's Gym and Da would train me in the ancient art form. A score would play loudly in the background, from some classic film, and the audience would know things were getting better. The people in the theatre would know that I was going to be okay.

I would be okay.

Tuesday showed up and with the gym address written down I jumped into a cab. I offered, in the best Mandarin a new guest of the country could, the name and the address of the gym.

The heavyset driver nodded in a universal gesture of understanding as I caught the long hair coming from a mole on his cheek. This was good luck.

His palms were sweaty and I wondered why he didn't crack the window to let a touch of winter in. I wouldn't have minded the crisp air because I could already smell the bowl of soup he ate for lunch on his breath.

Da said Gold's Gym was a ten minute drive from my house so 20 minutes into our journey I was reconsidering the lucky mole hair.

The taxi driver was going slowly so I mentally accounted for that difference. With more effort than what seemed necessary to exert in a vehicle with power steering the driver exited the freeway.

The volume of the song playing in the cab seemed to steadily increase as we zipped around. At first it sounded like old music from far away but then I realized I was on that side of the planet. I was living in that faraway place.

The driver pulled up in front of a newly-constructed warehouse. The cranes were still in place as if the construction had been completed that morning. He turned back with a confident smile having completed his task successfully. No gym was in sight.

My forehead started to reveal my anxiety with tiny drops of moisture. I patted the pockets of my jeans in search of help. My cell phone was on my bedside table. I had no business card and no help of any kind available to summon. He sensed my angst as I gestured for him to turn the music down. Gestures were all I had, now.

He didn't respond to my request about the volume and instead repeated the sentence I'd said to him thirty-two minutes earlier. He was right, it sounded the same. Then he pointed out the window and repeated it again. Obviously, I needed more time with Ginger.

I shook my head side-to-side unsure what else to do, then pointed my finger forward. The taximeter was running and I had only a little extra *yuan* in my pocket. He seemed to understand I'd gotten it wrong.

I decided if we didn't see the gym within the next few minutes I could ask him to take me to the kindergarten. I could get us there, which was half the distance back to the District.

He took side streets and front streets. I saw elderly women in pajamas walking through alleys. I witnessed men huddled around board games in parks and on corners. There were street vendors roasting sweet potatoes in garbage cans and a low haze dangled in the air.

None of it, well except for the smog, looked familiar. I desperately tried to remember something -- anything Da mentioned about the gym's location but nothing came to mind. With the child lock still on my windows, my breath tightened, and all I could think about was fresh air.

Another twenty minutes of driving around and I watched the meter register my last bit of money. I'd decided against trying to borrow from someone at the kindergarten knowing it was well past school hours and likely no one was there.

The school was in a residential neighborhood and I couldn't imagine trying to get a neighbor to help me out either. *How would I explain that I needed a temporary one-day loan for a taxi driver?* Surely the amount I'd just spent on fees would exceed what they could loan me.

I motioned for the driver to pull over at the next street light. I'd walk. My shirt was soaked through with sweat. I was lost and there was nothing to do but walk.

After the driver refused my third attempt to pay him I got out and walked to the street crossing. For a minute I felt badly that much of the time in the backseat I'd thought the driver was trying to take the long way to cheat me. Now, I saw, he had been trying to help. *I wanted my faith back.*

Eventually I found my way to the gym. It wasn't that day, but four days later. That day I walked until finally I stumbled into a travel agency that graciously called LeeAnn for me. She picked me up a few minutes later. LeeAnn knew her way around and I still depended on her whether I liked it or not.

Traveling around Shanghai in a taxi was actually quite easy if you handed the driver a business card written in Chinese. I knew that now, but I managed to take the longer route to most lessons in China.

After a week or two the initial inconvenience and soreness of working out wore off. I started to look forward to the gym after work. I even began punting my afternoons with Ginger. As much as I valued communication I just didn't have a knack for Mandarin.

Recently Ginger had started inviting friends to our conversations as well and I'd sit there for over an hour as they caught up. The cost to me was always the same, with or without the personal attention, and I started to resent trying to learn Mandarin through osmosis.

In the end, I chose Gold's Gym over Ginger. My homesickness was dominating the real estate between "being present" and perpetual negotiations around past regrets and future concerns. I needed to work out more than I needed to talk.

I walked to the stationary bike and entered thirty minutes on its digital clock then draped the scratchy white gym-provided towel over it. I didn't need to watch the timer slowly ticking down in front of me. I already had old smoke in my lungs to haggle with -- that would be enough.

I caught a reflection in the mirror in front of my bike of a woman I went to college with in Chico. I couldn't believe there was actually a familiar face. We hadn't been close friends but she instantly felt like one.

Overjoyed, I got off my bike and walked over to ask what it was that brought her to the other side of the world. But as I approached her I noticed she was Chinese -- not my friend from home. This was happening so often lately that I began to question my mental health again.

I rode for as long as I could which lasted about 40 minutes. I decided next time I would bring a book or some other sort of distraction. I sauntered into the lady's room and opened my locker.

The gym felt just like America. Things were sterile and organized with space everywhere uninhabited by people. A couch and cozy chairs sat empty. Magazines left on the middle benches remained untouched. I walked over to the hot tub and although empty and inviting followed my hunger pains to the hot shower instead.

Right across from the gym there was a Thai food restaurant. It was up the stairs from a little taco joint. I'd been thinking about taking some red curry home tonight.

So, with damp hair and gym sweats on I walked in. I asked if I could order something to go and the woman nodded as she walked me to a table to sit down. I pointed to the curry.

I assumed she seated me because I looked tired. But, she hadn't understood "to go". It didn't matter to me. Since I was staying, I ordered a glass of wine, too.

The white rice arrived first with a few peppers garnishing the plate.

The Huang family had already taught me to eat the rice last so I took a bite of a red pepper garnishing the tray to ward off my hunger. After a small first bite, I launched the rest of the pepper into my mouth.

Immediately, my eyes started to water and I realized my mouth was taken by a tingling sensation. Within seconds, the discomfort had intensified to the point where I was physically uncomfortable.

I felt my heartbeat pick up and reached for a glass of water at the edge of the table. I was pretty sure it was left there from the previous guests but I didn't care.

As soon as the water hit my mouth the burning exploded. *Calm down, nobody dies from eating a hot pepper.*

The waitress walked over with my glass of white wine. Before she got to the table I stood up and pulled the glass from her hand. It was rude and I tried to apologize with my eyes as I gulped it down. My palms were sweaty and the burning continued to intensify. The waitress now seemed to understand my distress.

I lunged for the little plastic tray of sugar packets at the end of the table. I ripped a few packets open and poured them in my mouth.

"Red pepper -- no eatty only looky".

This was most likely her attempt to be comforting but I needed relief not comfort.

"Is there something that will help?"

Her eyes widened with fear, "Allergic?"

Before I had a chance to answer she was back in the kitchen. I sat down remembering how many times in my life I'd passed out when in physical distress.

A moment later, a cook walked out from the kitchen with a coconut. He had a knife in hand and when he reached my table, he sliced it in half, tipped my head back, and dumped it into my mouth. There was a little relief amid the mountain of embarrassment.

When I got home I got into the shower to cool off. I couldn't even let the water hit my face it was so sensitive. My lips and eyes were swollen and there were sizable red splotches all over my face and neck. I needed sleep, if for no other reason, than to hide.

I wandered out into the living room, crawled on to the couch and put in my bootlegged copy of Anna and the King. It was the film I watched to relax when the Weather Channel wasn't an option.

I fell into a deep sleep.

God spoke.

"Breathe in the sweet air daughter, as you do take notice of every living thing around you -- the grass, the air, the trees. Notice the birds flying overhead. Notice even the quiet. All of life is connected. All of life is perfectly intertwined in a precious balance of give and take, of birth and death, of you and everything. Breathe in and be free of fear, my daughter. All things are exactly as they should be. There is only love and you are love."

I was a blue poppy planted in the middle of a field of blue poppies. My entire family was there. We were all blue poppies. The sun was a bright orange and in unison we bent our necks backward to open our faces to its warmth. I felt connected to each of the flowers, just as I felt connected to the earth and the sun, the grass and the breeze.

I was not conscious of days coming and going but I sensed that time was indeed passing by. I spent the hours leaning my head back, alongside my family, as we opened our mouths to drink up the mighty rays of light. It was warm. I felt safe and content.

Then, suddenly, a storm took over the orange sky. Both of my parents bowed their heads as my siblings followed. I knew to watch, as I couldn't recall having lived through a rainstorm before. They crouched down. So, I did the same.

As a massive gust of wind arrived my mother leaned toward me and said, "Honey you are not safe here. It's time you learn that you are different than the rest of us. You will not survive this storm. You see, we are blue poppies and the Creator planted us in this big blue poppy field. Together we can withstand the rain and the winds as our small roots are tucked deep inside the earth's crust."

The wind picked up and I felt a chill pass through me. "I know, mama, me too. I'm safe beside you," I pleaded.

"Honey, the Creator dropped you in our field on your first day so we raised you like a blue poppy but you are not like the rest of us. You are not a flower. See, look here...," she pointed to her petals.

"Unlike our petals your petals are covered in feathers. Your petals can take you places."

I looked down at my petals and my mother continued, "Look at your roots. They are not stuck in the ground. You can move them about."

What she was saying looked true although I had never noticed it before.

"Mama, I'm scared. I don't like what you're saying. Please don't say those things anymore. I want my petals to be like your petals. I want my roots to be like your roots. I want to stay here and wait out the storm until the sun returns and we lean our heads back together and drink up the sunshine."

"I know you do, sweet daughter. At first, I wanted that too. But you must use your petals and your roots the way the Creator intended you to. It is not for us to change. If you stay here you will surely die, if not from this storm than from a broken heart."

I felt raindrops against my face and was grateful the sun had gone away.

"Move your petals darling -- up and down -- go find shelter. When the time is right you will come back to the blue field of poppies and visit with us. We will love you just as we always have. For we have always known who you really are and we love you that way -- it is time you do the same."

My mother ducked to avoid another massive gust of wind and rain. She lifted her eyes and then with them begged me to leave.

"It's okay. You'll be okay, I promise. If you use your petals to fly you will see that there are many others just like you, you are not alone. You will never be alone. You are a bluebird, sweet daughter. Be brave and fly."

I wasn't sure what was happening but I trusted my mom. Somehow I knew she was right. I couldn't make sense of it all yet. So, I did as she instructed and moved my petals as fast as I could until, alas, a great gust of wind lifted underneath me and I was in the sky. I was flying.

I was more scared than I'd ever been in my life. I looked down at the field and watched the rain splash against the earth. I saw each family member I had grown to love still rooted down there. They were safe even amid the storm.

The last thing I saw was my father watching me leave. He kept his head up even with the mighty storm hitting his face. I knew he wanted me to see his unconditional love.

I found a tree to sit in to wait for the storm to pass. All I wanted was to fly back to my family and pretend to be a flower again. But no one could pretend that anymore. I knew the truth now.

I woke up when my leg fell off the couch and hit the floor. The dream was gone. My face was still splotched and now visibly swollen. The remnants from the fresh dream weighed on my heart.

Was that God talking to me? Was it okay to be me after all of this pain and suffering in an attempt to be different?

I spent the next 24 hours in bed. I wanted to get up but couldn't. It wasn't the reaction to the hot pepper but the dream that had robbed me of all my energy.

Every part of my body ached, every thought hurt. I tried to recall what had led me to China in the first place and the first thing that came to mind was Christy.

Part Two

I've always come to you, as I am
I've prayed to you, as I am
I've loved you, as I am

If that is not enough
Then I am not enough
For I am -- only as I am

Unanswered Prayers

Lies always make way for the truth, eventually.

It was a rare rainy day in our sunny Southern California town. I went to the library for shelter and to warm a bit. I had a few hours to blow before basketball practice so I fumbled through the aisles and stumbled upon a collection of letters from Abigail Adams to her husband. This would do. I was a hopeless romantic after all.

I sat at a table next to the aisle in case I wanted to go back for seconds. I opened the book and felt its spine crack slightly inside of my palm. A musty scent escaped the thin yellowish pages. I took a deep breath and imagined Abigail sitting in front of a fire crafting letters to her lover, friend and husband; a man the rest of the world called President. As the rain tapped on the roof of the library I tiptoed into the past.

Students popped in and out of the old book repository playing tag with the rain. With each gust of laughter that broke open the massive doors, I looked up. When finally I acknowledged that no real consumption of Abigail's prose was taking place I set the book down.

Just as I did the library door swung open again and a rush of yellow and brown cheerleading outfits with giggling faces filled the entrance. The cheerleaders were soaking wet and wiping the rain off frantically as if it might bite.

I noticed Christy right away. She stood there beside the squealing girls and calmly brushed a few lingering raindrops off her forehead. Her long blond hair and blue eyes took ahold of my attention. She took a couple steps toward me.

Just when she was close enough to touch, she turned around and pressed her back against the table I was sitting at. She smelled clean like Downy dryer sheets. She felt like happiness right before it becomes laughter.

I must have made a sound because she turned her head over her shoulder and said, "Oh, I'm sorry, did I get you wet?"

I couldn't speak.

"Hey, I know you. I see you and your twin playing basketball after school, in front of your house. I live right around the corner."

I forced a constipated smile to the corner of my mouth.

"We should hang out sometime."

I tried a few times but formulating a sentence was not possible. My tongue was stubbornly pressed to the top of my mouth.

Christy didn't seem to notice and offered instead, "Ok, see you later then. You're Alexa, right?"

I managed to nod.

Christy and I instantly became friends and like most teenage girlfriends we were inseparable. We dressed alike -- talked alike -- laughed alike and found every reason we could to spend our free time together.

At the Friday night football games I watched her move with ease and happiness as if oblivious to the violence just inches behind her. The young boys colliding in the background disappeared for me too.

With Christy's jumping and shouting "Go Eagles," the base of my stomach seemed to fill with millions of butterflies. It was a feeling that confused and terrified me. But even with the confusion I couldn't take my eyes off of her.

Every once in a while she would glance in my direction and hold my eyes for an extended second. In those moments, the butterflies escaped my stomach and I felt millions of tiny wings fluttering, back and forth, inside of me. All I could do was hold my breath until she looked away.

One evening after a game I went back to Christy's house. This had become our Friday night ritual. We hit the playroom and dove in front of her family's vintage jukebox. I pressed all of the numbers that corresponded with Michael Jackson songs as I descended to the floor beside her.

She smelled good. She always did. She smelled so good. We laid there with our legs crossed in the air behind us for as long as our bodies could resist the desire to intertwine. When it became too difficult to stay apart she pressed her soft cheek against mine. I felt warmth cascade over me. It was dizzying. I had imagined, no less than a thousand times, the way her skin would feel. But it was even softer than I had imagined.

Then I felt her lips brush across mine. There was a faint sweetness to her breath. Her lips were soft and moist. I'd been kissed before but nothing felt like this. She started to kiss me slowly and I knew this was who I was.

Christy and I fell in love the way all teenage girls do, madly and completely. The tortuous difference was the absolute secrecy. It was a topic we refused to discuss with anyone -- even with each other.

Well, at least, I refused to. Christy didn't seem to care what anyone thought about our love -- including God. She loved me and wanted to be together.

Although I wanted to be with her I was tortured by my thoughts. To add even more conflict in my mind, Christy didn't seem to be enduring the same struggle. *Why were the fears of burning in Hell only inside of my mind?* All I could feel was angst when I thought of her.

I chose denial. I was nowhere near ready to accept being gay. If accepting being a lesbian was at the shore, I was on the ocean's floor. Where I was it was dark and cold and years from reaching the sunlight.

Remarkably, even amid the secrecy, and my internal torture, our love for one another was strong enough to survive for a little while. It was the truth after all, and the truth craves oxygen.

If ever a moment of courage arose, I pushed away my fears and chose Christy. I momentarily silenced the fear of God's wrath and society's rejection.

But it never lasted long. I was in constant negotiations with God. *If you just give me one more day I will try harder to be someone else. I'll start over tomorrow. I'm sorry, please forgive me.*

I hardly considered my parents' reaction, as just the idea of their disappointment sent me into a bout of self-denial for weeks. I would emerge with self-induced emotional bruises and wounds that took months to heal. Then, I would swear off all correspondence with Christy, until I couldn't stand missing her anymore.

How Christy was so patient with me I will never know. We vowed, in our secrecy, not to love other people and that seemed enough for both of us for a while.

In high school years we were together, off and on, forever. Three years to be exact. Part of me thought we might actually make it. I didn't know how, but I thought if she was my soul-mate we would find a way.

But as my graduation neared and new uncertainties about college came to the foreground my conversations with God intensified. The more those conversations increased the more certain I was that I'd never be able to accept being gay.

"I'm sorry. I can't live like this. I'm so sorry."

"I'd rather die than lose you," Christy cried with tears I couldn't show.

"I can't do this anymore, Christy. I can't be responsible for your eternity in Hell. No love is worth millions of years of suffering."

"That's a lie. Those are lies, Alexa. Those are fucking lies. Don't do this to us."

"I'm sorry."

"Why would you believe in a God like that? A God who would send His own children to Hell because of how they love? It's a lie. You just don't love me. Just say it."

I did love her as much as I could love anyone with a heart filled with fear.

Christy turned to another lover. For which, I never blamed her. I turned to God.

I prayed all of the time. I begged and pleaded and prayed. I prayed to be straight. I decided I'd rather not love than to live in eternity, alone. I wasn't about to tell my parents the truth. *Why should they suffer, too?* This was my burden to bear. This wasn't their fault.

So, day and night, I talked to God. When I wasn't praying I was trying to please Him. I was fixated on being a good person. I listened to my parents. I didn't experiment with drugs or alcohol. I was kind to strangers. And, I prayed God was noticing.

But even after ending things with Christy and all my good behavior -- nothing inside of me seemed to change.

In desperation, I went the wrong direction. I turned to the Old Testament for help. It was filled with a brutal God. I needed that God. I needed more fear. A God who could strike his children dead with plagues and diseases might help change me.

There was a problem with this source of fear though. Since I had been raised a Christian, I believed the God in the Old Testament changed after Jesus Christ.

My post-Christ understanding made it difficult to accept that the words in the Old Testament about homosexuality were still true when so much of that text had been abandoned after Jesus.

There was only one solution left in my terrified adolescent mind. I'd have to accept that even after Jesus, God could hate me for being gay. I needed New Testament proof that Jesus didn't love me as I was.

So after months of searching I found a Jesus that might hate me for being a lesbian. Actually, I didn't. What I found was a Jesus that had the ability to be upset for no discernible reason. I needed that kind of Jesus to prove my point. I was desperate, and clear thinking was the first sacrifice made in that state of mind.

As it went on that April day, somewhere in the middle of the world, a fig tree sat under the sun as Jesus walked by. Jesus with very hungry and grew furious to realize that the fig tree bore no fruit for Him to eat. In His anger He cursed the tree to an early death.

I empathized with the fig tree. It no more created itself and chose when to bear fruit then I created myself and chose to be gay.

It was written right there in the Book of Matthew, a story which proved that if Jesus had enough anger to condemn an innocent fig tree to an early death then I must be in danger too.

I didn't know that Jesus never once spoke about homosexuality. I didn't know that He spoke about everything important to his Father and yet never mentioned it -- not once.

Naturally I assumed homosexuality had been the core of His message. Most likely, the subject of the majority of His talks. It must've been, if not, why had all this attention been given to it? Why would His followers judge and condemn God's gay children to a life without Him? Why were we being treated as the scapegoat no longer required to please a harsh God who no longer existed?

The internal suffering that might've been saved had I known that humans wrapped their own characteristics around God like a wet paper towel was enormous. But, none of that was clear to me in high school; in my life God was like an angry old man who happened to live in the clouds.

In no time, I started to believe that my fate would be the same as the fig tree if I stayed gay. *Death was coming.*

There was a Murder

Fear is the path away from self.

There was a murder while I was in high school. It wasn't mine. It was my best friend's brother.

Michael was the only person, other than my twin sister, who I'd confided in about my sexuality. He was my best and closest friend.

"I love Christy."

"What are you, in a fight or something?" Michael asked from the corner of his mouth, never looking up from the homework we were working on.

"Not exactly," I replied, mentally trying to talk myself out of the recent decision to tell him the truth.

"You guys will make up. You two always fight and make up, Lex."

I appreciated his insight and remembered why he was my best friend. It didn't occur to Michael I already knew how girls acted with each other.

"No, I mean, I am in love with Christy."

Michael was silent for what felt like too long for acceptance to follow.

"Oh. Oooh. Ooooh, you do?" He finally offered, blinking a few too many times. "Wait, why are you crying?"

"I've never said those words out loud. Not even to her."

"It's ok, Lex. It will be okay."

Michael didn't say much to me. Instead, the following day he came over after school and handed me a mixed tape.

He had copied The Pretenders song "I'll Stand by You" to both sides as many times as it would hold. I'd never heard the song before and played it over and over again as we fumbled through our biology homework.

For a moment I believed him that things would be okay. If Michael could feel this way toward me, maybe, so could my parents. And, if they could, maybe, just maybe, God could love me too.

"Oh, why you look so sad? -- Tears are in your eyes -- Come on and come to me now -- Don't be ashamed to cry -- Let me see you through -- 'Cause I've seen the dark side too -- When the night falls on you -- You don't know what to do -- Nothing you confess -- Could make me love you less -- I'll stand by you -- I'll stand by you -- Won't let nobody hurt you -- I'll stand by you."

I looked up to tell him how safe I felt when he was near. I wanted him to know his friendship lived in the middle of my heart and that nothing earthly could ever change that.

I started to tell him but it was late and he was packing up his things to go home. It didn't seem right to rush such a confession so I held it for another time.

"Michael! Are you ok? What's wrong?"

All I could hear was crying.

"Michael, what's wrong?"

"Ron's been murdered."

I had the tape he made me playing in my bedroom and turned it down to hear him say it again over the phone,

"Ron's dead."

I temporarily stopped worrying about my own death and took care of Michael.

I had no idea who OJ Simpson was and didn't care what people thought of him. Ron was gone and Michael and his family needed room to grieve. But there was no room left in our little town once the camera crews and bright lights arrived.

It turns out that when somebody famous commits a crime everyone else fades into the shadows. I felt helpless. I couldn't do anything to protect Michael. Nor could I, or anyone who loved his family, stop the world from turning Ron's death into a race war, media circus and national obsession.

So instead, I tried to find a little space so that Michael could breathe. Most days after school we'd head to the cemetery or go for a long car rides with the ocean beside us. We'd blast music and pretend everything was okay.

Every once in a while Michael talked about the murder trial and how his family was doing. They needed to know that although nothing could bring Ron back at least OJ's life of freedom would be taken. We had no doubt that OJ would be convicted -- until the day the jury deliberated for less than four hours -- and he wasn't.

The shock of the verdict made my fear of death roll in like a storm. Now that a death -- an actual murder -- had happened, God's wrath became my mental obsession. I started to avoid cracks in the sidewalk. I increased my prayers. Death was real now.

If there was grace during those high school days it was the illusion I could manifest on the outside. I coveted the illusion that I could convince everyone into thinking I was happy and straight. After all I desperately wanted to be.

I survived by creating two different worlds to orbit in. On the outside I was at the top of my class academically. I held leadership positions in our student government and led after-school clubs focused on world humanitarian issues. I led my basketball team to championships and was consistently named one of the top players in the region. I learned to be the very best at everything I could control.

I wanted to succeed in the terms the world could understand. I received awards and accolades that brought pride to my parents, grandparents and all those who loved me. I got recruitment letters from universities throughout the United States asking me to study with them and don their basketball jersey.

On the outside I fought to protect everyone I loved, especially my mother and my father, from the shame of a daughter who was "like me".

On the inside, I ached. I broke apart from the lies, guilt and shame. I began each morning with a promise to God to be someone else, and by nightfall I was on my knees praying for forgiveness for having failed miserably.

Scared Straight

You can almost scare a child straight, but more often than not you'll just scare them to death.

Located up the chest of California is a big town-little city, known to most for its Sierra Nevada beer and the right arm of NFL sensation Aaron Rodgers, but for me it was the home of California State University, Chico, where I had been recruited to play basketball.

Christy would be left behind. I would start over. I would reboot my sexuality. *I'd give that idea one last try.* I would love only Jesus. Well, Jesus and that orange round leather ball.

The moment I checked into my dorm room on the second floor of Lassen Hall I vowed to walk the walk. To be born again would certainly provide the peace I needed. I didn't need love.

I didn't need love. I didn't need love, well not the kind that came from someone else -- only Jesus -- just God.

I had such a loving family and circle of friends. No kiss or touch or sip or impulse or thought or deed or act was worth eternal damnation after all.

I would speak in tongue or go door-to-door to spread the Good News. I went to church every week. I joined campus clubs for worship. I prayed nonstop. I re-read my Bible.

But three years into college and countless nights on the bathroom floor with a sickness that comes from self-hatred, and I was still *me* in the morning. God must've been busy with something else. He wasn't listening to my prayers.

I decided that if God didn't have time to change me than Daniel would. If sexuality was a choice -- I was choosing straight.

Daniel walked into the Chico State gymnasium one afternoon when I was shooting around. He'd just finished water polo practice and was walking through as a shortcut to his car parked in the back of the building.

The ball bounced over to him and somehow we started up a conversation. Those hours turned into weeks, those weeks into years.

For all the love I couldn't offer myself I created space for Daniel to fill. He knew who he was and accepted it. I wanted that peace. I wanted to love him the way he loved me. And, I tried too with every bit of my heart.

Any warning signs about what I wasn't feeling were shut down. If on a quiet evening after our homemade dinner some uninvited truth emerged from the pit of my stomach, as we were sitting on the couch watching a basketball game, I turned up my self-talk. I lied. And, I believed them. It was easy to believe them because I desperately wanted the lies to be true.

"I will love you forever, Alexa."

"Me too. I will too," I offered hoping that I would.

Unfortunately, I learned after I'd made too many real promises to Daniel that you can't pretend to be someone else without breaking your own heart and the heart in front of you. I trusted him and he trusted me. And, in the end, I was lying to both of us.

It ended badly. Lies always end badly even when you don't know you're weaving them. I couldn't make myself straight any more than a straight person could pretend to be gay.

Without Daniel the internal civil war that was brewing my entire life started to creep to my edges. Like anyone trapped in the silo of self-rejection I created another option to self-acceptance. I convinced myself I could hold things together, even without God or a boyfriend, as long as I had basketball.

Basketball at the Division II level was a full-time job and would be enough to distract me. I lived in the gym. I only left to eat and go to class. I put everything else away. I knew the game would save me. It always had in the past.

"Alexa, grab the pennies, would you?" a teammate hollered from across the gym.

I wrapped the yellow net jerseys around my arm and walked over to the team. We divvied up the jerseys and stepped out on to the hardwood floor to stretch a little.

I'd torn apart the ligaments in my right knee in high school and knew the importance of warming up, but it was already 100 degrees in the Sacramento Valley, so I rushed through the stretch. I was ready to play.

Halfway through the game I had an open shot on the baseline when my defender slammed into the side of my knee. The ligaments inside of my shell exploded. It was my left knee this time.

My season was over before it began. My reliable distractions were dissipating, quickly. The game was over. And, with it, the only part of me that I liked was gone.

Like any real shame the moment I stopped moving it emerged from the base of my stomach and took me over. I had hundreds of lies, half-truths and unrealistic expectations to break down. I had regret and guilt to break down. I had years of fear to break down. So, I did -- I broke down.

I couldn't manage to deny it any longer. I left Chico State and went home to Agoura Hills to heal. I needed to go home. I wanted to be near my mom.

Amid the crisis it never occurred to me that accepting who I was would end my suffering. I clung to the belief that the suffering was because of who I was. I believed the suffering was because I was gay, not because I was denying it. *How many more years would it take to understand that accepting myself meant ending the pain?*

"What'd you feel like right after Ron was murdered?" I asked Michael late one night when things started to unravel. "I mean physically what happened?"

"It was really scary. You know what it was like. You were there. What's going on, Lex? Are you okay?" Michael gently replied.

"I just don't feel like me. I don't understand what's happening. I can't eat. I can't sleep. Yesterday I got out of the shower and looked in the mirror and I swear I didn't recognize my own face. I'm scared. I'm scared this won't pass."

Michael didn't say much but I felt his friendship inside of my heart. I would find it there again when I was ready. We had been through so much together. I hung up the phone and got a little sleep.

In the morning I asked my mom if anyone in our family was crazy.

"Not that I know of honey."

"Well, what about on dad's side? Certainly someone in the family is insane."

"Honey, what's wrong?"

"I need to talk with someone. I think I might be losing my mind."

No one I knew went to therapy. No one I knew, even knew anyone that went to therapy (well at least anyone) that would admit to it. But I was pretty sure I was losing my mind and a stranger sounded like a safe place to start.

I looked in the yellow pages and found the name of a guy in Simi Valley. I called and let it ring a while, until finally an answering machine picked up as the call-waiting buzz rang through.

I promised myself to call back the therapist, then clicked over to learn that death was near again.

I threw a few things into my worn-out basketball bag and asked my mom to drive me to the Burbank Airport. I was terrified of going back to Chico. I hadn't resolved any of my internal chaos and wasn't sure how I'd deal with more pain.

The facade I'd managed to maintain during the earlier stages of my life had cracked into a million little pieces. Even if I wanted to put it back together there was no way to do it.

As the plane took off I recalled the phone call, four years earlier, which had led me to Chico in the first place.

"Hello"

"Hi this is Mary Ann Lazzarini -- 'M.A.' I'm the head women's basketball coach for Chico State."

I covered the bottom of the phone and turned to my identical twin for help. "Where's Chico?"

"I don't know," Alisha responded.

Then she yelled into the kitchen, "Mom where is Chico?"

I slugged her in the shoulder with the hand holding the phone. "Shhh, this is the basketball coach there."

We'd been recruited across the nation but had finally settled the week before on the University of California, Santa Barbara. The Los Angeles Times had run a short article on the two of us and another pair of identical twins. It was all set; we were going to play on the coast. We both craved the ocean and the game in the opposite order.

I got back on the call and offered that information to M.A. I heard my mom provide some geographical insight from the kitchen while tending to her homemade lasagna but I couldn't hear anything over M.A's recruitment pitch.

"Okay, well that's good, Alexa. I love the ocean too. But come for a visit anyways. The ocean is just a few hours from here. I'd love to show you around our little town even if your hearts are set on an ocean view."

I covered the phone again and whispered to Alisha, "It must be in the desert somewhere. It sounds hot. No ocean apparently."

Somehow with her optimism and charm M.A. convinced us to take a trip to Chico. As we drove from Sacramento to Chico we tried to figure out who would choose a place with such short buildings and limited shopping malls. It was so different than what we'd come to know and love during our youth.

After we unloaded our bags at the Vagabond Hotel we visited all the must-see spots with M.A. I was instantly sold. I wanted a new start. I wanted to be someone else and this was that chance.

"Do you have jersey number 31 available?"

"Sure, Alexa."

"I'm in."

There was a little more to my decision but in the end everything inside of me trusted M.A which made my choice easy. I sensed that she would be the mentor I needed for the upcoming chapter of my life. And, she had been.

In the years that passed, I'd gone from playing for her to coaching with her. We'd become good friends.

"When I'm done, you and Alisha, you'll take over the program."

I smiled. I knew that was the plan but I didn't like the idea of her retiring anytime soon. She had way too much left to give.

But, she knew something I didn't.

She was dying.

When the Southwest plane hit the tarmac an overly bubbly stewardess started singing about slightly shifted luggage. I wondered how she could be so cheery when M.A. was dying. *Did she know how fragile life was?*

I drove straight from the Sacramento Airport to Enloe Hospital. The florescent lights in the hospital hallways were harsh and I was grateful for the rain against the windows that I could see when walking by open hospital room doors.

I wanted it dark. I wanted it completely dark so that no light dare illuminate the truth inside of me or inside hospital room 23 off the Esplanade. M.A. was dying and there was no way to stop it.

The moment I walked into her room my emotional crisis felt like a skinned knee. I walked in and saw my mentor, my friend, lying there fighting to fill her lungs up with air. She looked up and I sensed her asking me to come closer.

"Stay here okay? You and Alisha. I'd like you here when I leave," Mary Ann whispered from her hospital bed. "I want you both to be here."

Of course that's what we did. We stayed beside her until she took her last breath.

Even at 49 years old and in great health before her diagnosis it didn't take long for M.A's body to stop working. Her heart fought until the end. She wasn't leaving without a fight. She loved the world too much to leave without a fight.

But pancreatic cancer doesn't fight fair. It's the guy in the alleyway that shoots you from behind on a dark night before you ever see him coming. There is never a chance to turn around and throw a punch. Pancreatic cancer doesn't lace up and meet you in the ring, it just pulls the trigger from the darkness and takes what it wants.

It was impossible to believe that only four years before those florescent lights guided me to her room, I'd been recruited to play basketball for Mary Ann's Chico State Wildcats.

Now she was dead and I was standing there looking at her lifeless body. My mind refused to see that her chest had stopped its slight rise and fall.

Finally a nurse walked back into the room and confirmed what the few of us in the room already knew -- Mary Ann's heart had stopped. My heart ached.

Lying on the couch in Shanghai remembering my past, thinking of M.A.'s death, made me instantly feel ashamed to be lying there with a cancer-less body, paralyzed by my own fear. I was tired of trying to find peace with God. I wanted to enjoy the time I had left.

Had I really needed to fly to China to understand this? Why had it taken me this long to see I was squandering the little time I had? How many times did I need this lesson? I crawled out of bed, drank a huge glass of water and got dressed.

I didn't know yet that what I needed was a little compassion toward myself. I needed to stop trying to shame or guilt myself into becoming a better person. But none of that was clear yet. I only knew what I knew.

When I walked outside my neighbors were outside my door as if to greet me. They knew something was wrong having not heard the water turn on or a single door open or shut in two days. Mr. Huang handed me a bowl of soup and some dried meats. I was grateful they cared.

Part Three

*I came here to walk alone
to find my own space
my own place in this world.*

*In this solitude I sought only God's company
looking to the ever-changing sky
the ever-moving tide
the ever-present fears inside my mind.*

*How magnificent it was
after so many days of silence
to hear a voice this morning
and know that it was God.*

For the Time Being

The truth craves oxygen.

The pale moon rose each night and I dreamed of being in the blue poppy field. Within each dream a storm arrived. I stood there stuck in the field with wings that I couldn't use yet. There was no shelter I could find refuge in. I didn't belong in the field but wasn't ready to accept being a bluebird. I didn't want wings. What I wanted was to be like everyone else.

After a long anxious night in the storm, I woke up with tears dried against my face. I couldn't remember crying, but the salt water had made my cheeks sticky. I wanted to go back to sleep but hated the thought of being in that field again.

Since it was Sunday I was without work, Tai Chi or language lessons, so I got up and made a pot of tea. I knew a movie could provide a temporary escape from my thoughts, so I flipped through my choices. When I did, the phone rang. I picked up, hoping it was Da.

Amanda and William were on their way to brunch at M on the Bund and wanted me to join them. I didn't have an appetite but sensed that being around people that had love in their hearts was a better idea than dwelling on my recent dreams.

"You don't look good mate," Amanda noted in her Australian melody. "You've got big dark circles under your eyes."

She was right. The dreams were keeping me up all night. I shrugged it off but at the last minute added that I'd been having nightmares, then immediately tried to take it back realizing my vulnerability.

"Well they are sort of like nightmares, I guess. It is hard to describe. I'm stuck in a field of flowers so it could be worse, I suppose."

Amanda changed the subject, uninterested in my vulnerability or lack thereof.

"Well we missed you at the kindergarten last week. I'm sorry to hear about the hot pepper incident. LeeAnn called and told us the story. Is it too soon to tell you we were in stitches imagining you with coconut dripping down your face?"

I instantly felt alone. No one in my life knew how much I was struggling just to get out of bed and go about my day.

"No, honestly, Lex, Sukanya really struggled without you. Will you be back tomorrow? You should come tomorrow, we're going to the indoor playground again."

I was grateful everyone at the school thought I was healing from a weird reaction to a spicy vegetable and not the demons floating around in my head. I feared the dishonesty, knowing lies have a way of coming to the surface at the most inconvenient times.

"Actually, I'm thinking of taking a short trip to Hong Kong before I head back to the school," I jabbed into the air.

"Definitely, Lex. It must be sorted. These nightmares mean something. Things like that fester up to a dodgy mess if you aren't careful." Maybe Amanda knew more than I realized.

William chimed in, "Eh, love, you eatin' that muffin?"

"No dear, go on!" Amanda replied.

"Great then!"

Lathering the muffin top with butter and jam William offered his first contribution to our conversation. "Here's an idea, Lex. Come over tonight. We'll pop in Priscilla Queen of the Desert, eat something good, sip a pint or two, and sort it out proper."

I sat there wishing they knew the whole story. I felt so alone. I was alone in America, and now a thousand miles away I was still alone with my fears. For a brief second I considered blurting out, *I'm gay. I just want you to know in case that changes anything.*

Also, I'm pretty sure God hates me for it. I'm gay and I've spent my life hating myself for it. I have been running from my sexuality like it was some goddamn disease. But I can't change who I am.

I am tired of being afraid. Take me now. God, do you hear me? Just take me now and let this part end. Hell can't be worse than this running.

I realized I was talking to God again and not paying attention to my breakfast company. They were tending to mimosas and didn't seem to notice.

"What should I bring?"

"Eh, nothing, mate. We've got it all," William mumbled keeping the omelet just barely behind his lips.

And they did. They had it all. They had what I'd been searching for my entire life.

The lights never go out in Hong Kong. It is technically China but feels different in every conceivable way. I wasn't sure why Shanghai had been deemed the Paris of the East when clearly Hong Kong had the Prada purse and matching shoes.

Aside from the stylish city folk and lines of fabulous clothing boutiques, there were beaches, diverse and flavorful restaurants, and *manners*. Unlike what I'd grown accustomed to in Shanghai, in Hong Kong people walking down the streets walked around you -- not through you.

It wasn't uncommon to hear *"Ni Hao"* or an occasionally "Hello" in English if you made direct eye contact with someone. And, people actually made direct eye contact. People in Hong Kong formed lines and waited patiently within them. This behavior ran contrary to everything I'd been adjusting to on the mainland.

As I made mental notes of the myriad of differences on the island I ventured into one of the first hotels I saw and paid for a room for the week. I didn't want to feel rushed to resolve things by the checkout time looming in the morning. A week would give me plenty of time to sort things out. I needed time and I needed the ocean.

The hotel room was quite fancy. Chocolates rested on the pillows and a white robe and slippers peeked out of the closet. I unpacked my bag and neatly stacked the contents into piles on the dresser top. I decided a long walk on the beach was a splendid idea.

So, I rolled the bright yellow towel I'd picked up from a street vendor in Shanghai and a black sarong into my backpack, then sauntered out to the street to catch the red European double-stacked bus to Clear Water Bay.

"A few years ago a bunch of people were munched to death by sharks here," I heard coming from a young male voice with a muted British accent behind me.

I turned around visibly startled and splashing the water against my chest. I'd just waded out into the bay and into a thought about Mary Ann before the stranger's voice arrived. It was a gentle thought about her ashes being returned to the sea off the coast of Northern California.

"Come again?" I said spinning around as quickly as I could manage waist deep in water.

"Yeah, in '95 sharks swam up and killed people here, right in the middle of their afternoon swim."

I wondered why this guy thought this was appropriate information to offer a stranger but my curiosity trumped fear so instead of responding I started making my way out of the water. Just as I got up to the shoreline he yelled,

"Don't worry. They have shark nets out there now. Pesky things can't get through anymore."

Pesky things! These aren't mosquitoes we were talking about and how might a net hold off a shark that has spent 400 million years evolving in order to dominate the ocean?

I quickly resolved that this stranger could not be trusted. I walked back to my cheap towel and lay down. The last thing I needed was more fear. I was trying to purge decades of it as it was.

I didn't stay on the shore that long as my mood had been severely compromised by the Good Samaritan. Instead I caught the bus and went back to the hotel. My anxiety was off the chart so I washed my hands, folded and unfolded my clothing into new piles and crawled into bed.

I didn't make it back to Clear Water Bay. The busy streets were entertaining enough. I found things with little difficulty as my English was understood by just about everyone on the busy streets.

I stumbled into great Italian restaurants and bookstores. The clothing boutiques were equally delicious. The people were accommodating and I forgot for the time being I had so much shit still left to resolve.

After four days and with a mind brimming with distractions I called LeeAnn. "Come to Hong Kong for the weekend."

"That sounds wonderful."

"It's as incredible as you described it. And, I miss you."

I wasn't sure why I was calling LeeAnn from Hong Kong but old habits find ways back into the day easily when you aren't paying attention. I knew she'd come. I was getting bored alone and since I moved into my place in the French Concession I rarely saw her anymore.

"I'll meet you at Gaia on Queen's Road Central at 7 o'clock."

"Great. I'll see you there. Travel safely."

"Bye."

"Ciao."

I hung up the phone and felt a wave of anxiety rush through me. It had been a bad idea.

Instead of milling over it in my head I put my bathing suit on and walked to the front of the hotel to hail a cab back to the beach. I had the rest of the afternoon to fill before LeeAnn's arrival.

White Out

In a moment without intention that which we will never do is done; that which we will never say is said; that which is unbreakable is shattered.

The beach was packed. The first time I'd visited the water it had been a weekday. It appeared everyone planned beach trips on the weekend. I found a small-unoccupied cluster of sand and spread out the half of my towel that could fit.

It was much warmer than it had been on Tuesday so I rationalized the shark nets were constructed precisely to stop massive fish from getting through and a swim would be fine. If a shark did manage to penetrate the netting there were plenty other options in the water so I'd have time to escape.

The water was refreshing and I spent the next few hours wading around, forgetting entirely about the shark and LeeAnn.

What time is it? How could I have so quickly forgotten she was on the way? Great. I'll just head back to my hotel, shower up, and then meet her for dinner. It's gotta be close to 5 p.m.

It was 6 o'clock on the dot when I got back to my hotel. My face was red with sun. The activities I thought so little about back in the States had intertwined with my peace of mind on the road. I depended on them to occupy all my time. A shower was an activity; getting dressed; a meal was two or three hours of something to do.

It felt wrong to rush all the routines I'd come to depend on but LeeAnn would be there soon so I plowed through my rituals. I threw on my black Beatles t-shirt and a pair of blue jeans. They fit much tighter than I wanted so I kept the top button undone and the vintage shirt hanging out. I'd had the shirt for years and the little holes on my shoulder blade revealed its use. I thought of Christy and how long I'd been struggling to be someone other than who I was.

Then I glanced in the mirror and decided to throw a little product into my hair. I missed the hair products at home that knew how to handle my dark Greek curls. Instead it was a dollop of hotel lotion. It was hard to believe all of the concessions I had made to find freedom from my suffering.

So far, the adventure seemed to have only created more discomfort and a softer, wider human-suit to ride in. I promised myself I'd eat a salad for dinner and leave the pasta alone.

LeeAnn looked great. She'd been somewhere with the sunshine and wore its rays on her face and arms. It made her look younger than she was. She'd dressed much nicer than me and I suddenly wished I'd given more time to getting ready.

When LeeAnn was around I let her do the talking for us. She ordered a carafe of the house red, big salads and pastas. We drank one carafe that led to another and I started to actually feel relaxed.

LeeAnn had just returned from Thailand and was going on and on about the beauty of it there. All of the things that had begun to upset me in China about LeeAnn no longer seemed to matter. Her clinginess and insecurities almost felt endearing now. I couldn't put my finger on it but having her in Hong Kong felt so different than the dynamic we had in Shanghai.

In Shanghai, when LeeAnn and I were hanging out, I almost always talked about Isabel. The farther I had been from Isabel the more I missed the drama that relationship created in my life. It had been a beautiful distraction from dealing with myself.

Now, in Asia, there was so much self to deal with. I'd chosen instead to talk about the good and bad times with Isabel when hanging out with LeeAnn. I knew LeeAnn wanted more from me and keeping an ex-girlfriend between us seemed like a good idea.

But tonight I didn't feel like talking about Isabel. LeeAnn and I finished dinner and two massive carafes of red. She told me about adventures with Parkson at the kindergarten and caught me up on all the children. I felt more tipsy than normal and was grateful for the pasta (that I wasn't going to eat) helping to absorb the Italian adult grape juice in my stomach.

When we walked back to my hotel I offered LeeAnn the extra bed at my place. There was no reason for LeeAnn to get another room. I felt grateful to have something to offer her by way of hospitality. She was the entire reason I'd made it to Asia after all.

"Crash with me? We'll spend the money you save at boutiques in the morning. The shopping here is wicked!"

We no more than made it into the hotel room before we were ripping each other's clothes off. I had a fleeting thought about what this might feel like in the morning but quickly threw it off with the Beatles shirt.

A part of me was concerned about tomorrow but it faded as we pressed our skin against each other. We had sex all night long. The lingering tingle of wine made the minutes slip past. The sun was waking up by the time we finally fell asleep. As I shut my eyes I couldn't believe how long it had been since I'd slept with someone. With Isabel we rarely made love and one of us was always in tears.

Around 2 p.m. I finally got up. I had a terrible hangover and walked to the bathroom to rinse my face with cold water. Just as I dabbed dry the last bit of water from my forehead the undeniable sensation of regret ensued. *Why on earth would I have gotten naked with LeeAnn? This was a terrible decision. What had I been thinking?*

I heard the door handle turn, then realized I'd locked it after me.

"I'll be right out."

"You okay, Lex?"

"Yeah, just drank too much. I'll be out in a minute."

It took me thirty minutes to get out of the bathroom. I wanted desperately to get sick but couldn't manage to bring anything up. Instead I just pressed my face against the cold tile floor and let the earth spin with my regrets.

I decided there was absolutely nothing I could do to erase last night's decision. I would have to face the consequences eventually so I opened the door and walked out. LeeAnn was on the bed. She had a sweet look on her face and I felt badly for all the thoughts of regret I'd been having in the bathroom.

Dot at the Bottom
And, then an angel appeared.

Hong Kong nurtured the earlier thoughts I'd held in Hillary's Chico backyard of adventures on distant shores and the happiness constant movement promised in my mind. Shanghai hadn't delivered.

Complicating things by spending an evening with LeeAnn in Hong Kong just made my desire to keep moving that much stronger. I couldn't deal with another person's disappointment and pain right now. I had enough of my own to deal with.

On the plane trip back to Shanghai from Hong Kong I decided I'd finish what work I could with the kindergarten and find a new adventure. I didn't know yet that I was running from my suffering and that it would join me, with or without, an invitation.

I wondered if Qin would understand a decision to break my lease. I knew her father wouldn't. After eight months in Shanghai I was leaving them with a fully furnished IKEA flat and a bad feeling about Americans.

I needed to keep moving. LeeAnn would find a way to understand. If not, once she accepted that I was never going to love her in return, I knew that relationship would end. A part of me had always known what she wanted. I simply didn't have it to give.

When I returned from Hong Kong I pulled open a map of China. At the very bottom of the map there was a little island. I would later learn the Chinese call this land, "The End of the Earth". The map's fine print revealed the letters: H.a.i.n.a.n.

"Amanda, what do you and William think of Hainan?"

"Hainan?"

"Yeah, the little island at the bottom of China."

"Never thought about it before, Lex. Chinese folks vacation there. The rest of us head to Thailand."

I considered the suggestion and realized this was exactly the sort of trip that would prove my independence. Certainly China had been a good trial run, but I'd landed in the lap of ex-pats and an American boss. I needed to be able to travel alone, completely alone. Places without LeeAnn's help or Da's endless wisdom.

I let the children know I'd be leaving for a while. I wasn't completely convinced I could manage on my own and so I left a little room for the idea of my return.

I bid farewell to Ginger, Amanda, William and the Huangs. Then I dropped off my bootlegged collection of DVDs to Mr. Chen in hopes of easing the blow of my decision to go.

I stopped by the kindergarten to give a basket of edibles to Parkson. LeeAnn was at the kindergarten and managed to wish me safe travels. I knew I was hurting her by leaving now, but I had made no promises. I'd given what I could to China and to her.

I wasn't sure how I was going to manage without Da so I didn't think about him quite yet. It had been exactly eight months since I touched down in Shanghai and I knew I couldn't stay a moment longer.

The day before I left for Hainan, Amanda organized a little going away party for me at the school. All the children contributed to the patchwork. Dylan, Ling and Sukanya made me special collages. It was hard to leave but my mind was set on the End of the Earth.

At 6:30 a.m. the following morning Da picked me up and drove to the South Shanghai Train Station. Somehow I knew I'd never see him again.

I shoved the thought as quickly as I could down my chest but felt a familiar angst crawl to the edges of my tongue. I knew this feeling well. I tried to find my breath. I wanted Da to come with me.

By 8:00 a.m. the train station was teeming with Chinese men in suits getting ready to board the train to Guangzhou. I'd asked a coworker what the farthest south was that you could travel by train down the coast of China. Guangzhou had been her answer. I had no reason to doubt this information.

Boarding the train amid the masses of Chinese men was a new experience. Most of the men wore business suits and red cheeks. I wasn't sure what direction to go but there was little time to think inside the cluster of people. The swarm moved us from one place to another. By the time it started to break up we were inside the belly of the train.

I walked straight to the sleeper car number on my ticket and crawled onto the top bunk. The sheets were dirty but I didn't care. My eyes felt the weight of uncertainty and I wanted sleep. I noticed five other bunks inside of the room and prayed they'd remain empty as I dozed off.

I woke up abruptly with the smell of something odd right next to my nose. Firmly keeping my right eye shut, I slowly cracked my left eye open. A palm was extended in front of my face.

Inside the palm was a piece of dried meat. I shook off my shock and took the small gift from the hand, then opened my right eye and sat up.

A young man with inflamed red bumps all over his face was staring back at me. He was dressed in an old business coat and pants that had been made for a woman, yet hand-tailored for his slender teenage figure.

He was my only roommate during the train ride from Shanghai to Guangzhou. Since we didn't share any words in common, it was a quiet ride.

When I wasn't sleeping, I stepped across the narrow hallway separating our cabin door from the windows running along the side of the train, and watched the landscape of China pass by.

I practiced the breathing techniques Da had taught me so far. I let the changing scenery wash my mind with curiosity, knowing if I wasn't vigilant unpleasant feelings around uncertainty might easily emerge from habit.

The dusty gold fields were full of people bent over wearing hats that had the look of a lampshade. Rural China looked so different from the China I had come to know. After an hour or two of watching countryside pass by the slightly dirty train window, I would venture back to my bunk.

The train stopped frequently and most of the passengers got off to stretch their legs or grab food at the station. I, on the other hand, couldn't understand a single word of the overheard announcements and therefore decided to stay put. I couldn't risk being left in a bathroom in the middle of China's coast. I'd needed more time with Ginger and mentally critiqued my decision-making skills.

Twenty hours later the cranky train whined to a stop in Guangzhou. I grabbed my bag, exchanged a parting glance of solidarity with my roommate, and followed the crowd of people to a bus station. I needed to get a ride to the sea.

As the bus driver made his rounds dozens of people got on and off the bus. I was glued to the window in search of water and only pulled my eyes back to the inside of the bus once to notice a young boy get on alone. He couldn't have been ten years old yet.

The boy crawled onto the front seat then scooted his bottom to the seat's base making his legs stick out forward. He only took the bus one stop, then got off. It seemed odd that he was unaccompanied. I agreed with myself that he must live nearby. This was an infrequent event but something had required it.

At no point during the bus route did I see the ocean. *Where were the ships that were so eager to transport me to Hainan?* In fact, at no point did I see anything remotely resembling a dock or a portal to cross the seas.

When the bus driver finished his evening rounds he drove us back to the bus terminal. It was the same terminal that just hours before teemed with people. This time it was empty. We pulled into the garage, and the brown-eyed, gentle-faced driver turned around with a look of helplessness. I felt the same way.

It is an interesting feeling to be someplace where everyone else is home and you are lost. I hastily ripped a page from my journal and scribbled a picture of a boat on it.

He looked at my picture of the boat and offered no expression. I reached for it and he gave it back. I proceeded to draw a little island and an arrow from the boat to that island. I remembered Ginger's words of wisdom that pictures were to the Asians' eyes what words were to North Americans' ears. The memory brought comfort and I was certain the bus driver would understand the meaning of my drawing with the additions.

He looked at it again then took a loud gulp of oxygen into his smoke-filled lungs. He let out two short coughs then went back to staring straight into my eyes as if waiting for something.

There must be an explanation, right? This city must not be a port at all. I had traveled to the wrong place. I wasn't even convinced I was in China any longer. Maybe I had crossed the border into Mongolia while on the train. I lowered my eyes hoping to convey a sense of understanding that I knew whose problem this was.

As I stepped off the bus the sky darkened and rain arrived. I was lost. I was really lost. I needed to find a taxi if I had any hopes of getting a hotel room and out of the rain.

My backpack was stuffed full. The top of it rested about a foot above my head. The pack probably weighed 45lbs but with a bodyweight of 115lbs it took most of my strength to get it on and in a comfortable position.

I knew it was only one step on uneven ground or gravel that would send me to the ground. So I cautiously roamed around the streets, watching where I placed my feet, and searching for a taxicab through the raindrops.

I missed Da. He would have known exactly what to do in a moment like this. I thought of LeeAnn and Parkson and the recent familiarities that now felt far away.

Why did I always have to push things? A two-day trip down the coast of China, alone. Why?

The rain continued to drum against my shoulders and with no cabs in sight, I decided to rest. I found a curb and managed to get close enough to the ground to lean my backpack against it as I plopped down.

As I did, four men on motorbikes circled me. Each one was wet and looked as if he had been in search of me. Unlike the convenience of Internet and telephones in Shanghai, I was without lines of communication now.

In unison the guys jumped off their rides and approached me. I felt my skin tighten. This was still China, right? I wasn't being robbed. With a little gesticulating I realized they wanted to give me a lift. Gesticulation is the quickest point between two people who don't share a verbal language.

I realized the guys had not come together but were in fact competitors positioning for my foreign currency. After a little effort to get back to my feet I chose the bike closest to me and climbed on. I thought I caught my sleeve on the bike and looked down to set it free when I saw that it was a small child holding my soaking wet sleeve down.

"Not safe!"

"Not safe. Not safe."

Where the heck had he come from? Startled I jumped off the bike. The man on the bike snapped Cantonese at the young boy. I sensed being there was the only thing now between this young boy and the motorist's fist.

The little boy appeared to apologize to the man but did not back down from his stance to keep me off the motorbike. At less than four feet tall, he stood right in front of me. It was the boy from the bus.

It took a while but eventually all four bikers gave up, shrugging off the boy like a bad date not worth the time. The rain intensified. When it was clear I was safe from the bikers the boy ran off. I cried out for him to wait but he was gone.

I walked to a nearby building and sat down. The only energy I had was to wait out the rain. It had been more than 24 hours since I left my little flat in Shanghai. I hadn't eaten more than the dried meat and a Tigermilk bar. I wasn't prepared for this adventure. No wonder I hadn't told anyone what I was doing.

Just as I started to pull my thoughts together, to come up with a plan, the rain let up. I took it as a sign that clear skies were ahead. I needed something to believe in and that would do.

Just then a taxi came around the corner with the boy from before in the front seat. He must've run off to find a cab. My eyes filled with tears. I started to talk to him but he shook his head and responded in Cantonese.

I couldn't understand how he'd said so clearly "not safe" if he didn't have the basic greetings in English down. I handed him my drawing. He smiled and then said something to the driver.

It wasn't long before the three of us were making our way to the crust of the city. He knew I needed a boat to somewhere.

When we finally arrived at the port I handed the driver some yuan and grabbed my bag. The young boy was already on his way into the terminal. He walked up to a woman who looked to be in charge. The entire time he spoke to her she looked over at me as if I was someone to keep an eye on. I tried not to look away to prove her wrong.

After their conversation the boy turned to face me and opened up his right hand. With that I realized he must want to get paid and maybe this had been some elaborate scheme. This happens when you travel. I didn't care. I was safe. There was a ship. I would get to Hainan.

I walked toward the boy as he lifted his other palm wide open too. I took one more step toward him as I pulled out some yuan. He shook his head. He didn't want money. He smiled and was gone.

The lady in charge of tickets walked up to me and handed me a ticket to Hainan. It was completely written in Chinese.

I said in slow, quiet English, "Hainan?"

"Yes. Boy said, Hainan. Lucky you. Boat been cancelled many days. Bad weather. Lucky you. Today, ok." She continued, "You know, boy?"

"No," I confessed.

"No English. Boy no English. I speak English."

She was right. He hadn't appeared to speak any English. As I boarded the boat for a long ride to Hainan I wondered if angels came in the form I'd always imagined. Maybe they were here, among us.

Maybe God did love me after all.

Outside of my window I could see a tattered red flag carrying yellow stars. It flapped relentlessly in the wind at the front of the boat.

In spite of logic and planning and, quite frankly, common sense, I had managed to pay for a ticket and secure a private room on the ship to Hainan.

I stretched out on the cot and listened to the massive ship blow its horn as we left the Guangzhou Harbor. Dayu Peak faded behind us into dusk and we began our journey on the Pearl River, which would graciously escort us into the mouth of the East China Sea.

It was sunset. I settled in for the last bit of my journey to the dot at the bottom of China. As the only foreigner on board I took comfort in watching the river from my cabin window, not from the common areas.

The sea was calm even with the rain pounding against her face. Her name "Pearl" reminded me of a story Da told me one afternoon when the rain had interrupted our Tai Chi.

The yellow emperor was on his way back from K'un-Lun Mountains when he lost the dark pearl of Tao. He sent knowledge to find it but knowledge was unable to understand it. He sent distant vision but distant vision was unable to see it. He sent eloquence but eloquence was unable to describe it. Finally he sent empty mind and empty mind returned with the pearl. As the sun set in the Southern China sky I prayed I might finally be open to it all.

I slept in the little cabin for a while, maybe four or five hours before I woke up and felt like a monkey was jumping on my bladder. Even with the yellow emperor's story lingering in my mind I wasn't ready to face the other side of my cabin door. I felt emotionally hungover from the train ride and the bus ride and the uncertainty I was spinning in.

Alone on a cargo ship traveling through the South Pacific Ocean in the rain on my way to an island I had seen on a map, yet had never heard of before, justified the fear I was feeling. I didn't feel safe enough to leave the room so I crawled on to the little metal ledge holding the sink and peed. Desperate times call for desperate measures.

It was enough of a relief that I crawled back onto the cot and fell asleep again. I couldn't hear much in my little room beyond my thoughts. Was I still running from something? What was I searching for?

Eventually, the ship started to slow down and I sensed a port was near. We docked alongside numerous other well-used boats donning tattered China flags. We appeared to be in an industrial area where loading and unloading of cargo was the sole activity. The boats and ships sat at the back of large warehouses. As soon as I was certain we were done with the sea, I opened my short metal door.

A line of Chinese men were there to greet me. *Had they heard me pee in the sink? Was I going to be punished?*

I started to list in my mind all of the movies I'd seen where the protagonist puts herself in a terrible situation. It doesn't turn out well. *What was I doing here, all alone, at the bottom of China?*

It appeared that the three dozen or so men who had joined me on this trip across Pearl had been aware I was hiding inside my cabin.

They'd stood there as we docked knowing I'd have to come out eventually.

I lowered my head to walk by when an arm reached out and tapped me on the shoulder. In broken English he made out the words *tie, tan* and *tick*, then repeated them, *tie, tan, tick*.

He walked in front of me, leading me, to the stern of the ship. He looked back to make sure I was following. As soon as we got to the stern, he pointed to where he wanted me to stand. Another man pulled out a camera.

As if previously rehearsed the man standing behind me lifted his arms out to either side and exclaimed quite loudly, "I'ma king ga da world!"

The Heat of a Thousand Suns

At the bottom of the world
there is water
there is sunshine
there is life.

I wouldn't have believed it myself
had I not gone there
and found a flower
pushing through a crack
in the sidewalk.

It had been days since I left the Shanghai Train Station and in that time my 26th birthday snuck in. It would be my first birthday without my twin sister nearby to celebrate. A sense of sadness arrived but I was learning there was strength within that feeling. I was traveling on the other side of the world alone and although a bit lonely I was still managing all right.

Fortunately Sanya, Hainan was breathtaking and a great distraction. Since it had been so many hours since I had a conversation or a meal, and because it was my birthday, I decided the first person I caught smiling at me I'd invite for dinner.

The first person -- no exceptions. This would be my way of offering gratitude to all the strangers who helped me along my way. I thought of the little boy who had rescued me in the rain.

I grabbed my pack and went in search of a taxi. How constant and perpetual this task was while on the road. I put a CD that Da had loaned me in my portable CD player and started my walk.

Just as I started to finally relax I caught a taxi driver's face flash a smile a few feet away. His windows were down and the sticky island air was dancing in and out.

I returned his smile and motioned him toward me. I shut off my music just in time to catch the tail end of Bob Marley's "I Shot the Sheriff" coming from his car radio.

Since I had no idea where to go I grabbed the glossy brochures from the back pockets of the seats in front of me. A five-star hotel was needed. It was my birthday. Also, I'd need a concierge who spoke English to help translate my birthday dinner invitation.

There was a line of fancy hotels in Yalong Bay, so I pointed to one of them and handed it to the young man. He was Chinese but with sun-soaked skin making him a toasty brown. He took the brochure then turned up the music slightly. Another one of Bob Marley's songs played and I felt a deepening sense of gratitude that I'd made it to this little dot at the bottom of the world.

Even with the sticky air and smog-less sky, Chairman Mao still hung proudly from storefront windows watching. His face was so familiar to me I'd almost welcomed it before remembering the number of murders he'd been responsible for.

After about twenty minutes we pulled up to a very nice hotel. It looked nothing like the hotel I pointed to inside the brochure but I assumed the young man would take me to a location he knew which provided the necessary financial rewards of dropping off wayward travelers like myself. *What did I care?*

In any other situation I would have grabbed my pack from the trunk of the car and walked in but I wanted him to join me so I gestured for him to grab the pack. He understood. He'd seen that gesture a thousand times before.

A man who was no older than either one of us met us at the entrance. He was well groomed and in a perfectly pressed white suit and tie. The contrast in color against his skin made him look clean and attractive. He greeted us in both English and Cantonese. I wanted to take back my mental insistence to invite the first person that smiled at me to dinner and instead invite the second.

"My name is Tommy. I am here to make sure you have anything you might need to make your stay enjoyable."

I offered a slightly forced thank you. I knew his name wasn't Tommy and wondered why everyone made things so simple for Westerners.

"Would you mind asking my taxi driver to come back around 8 o'clock tonight?"

"Oh Ms. we have plenty of drivers here if you wish to go somewhere."

"I'd like it to be him if you don't mind."

Tommy turned to the driver and offered a handful of words I couldn't decipher. The driver turned and lowered his head and eyes slightly in acknowledgement.

"Xie, Xie, Tommy".

Once I got to my room I was absolutely exhausted. On the eighth floor I had a gorgeous view of the sea and just wanted to crawl in the fresh cold white sheets for the night. Then I remembered in a few hours my taxi driver would be back and waiting downstairs.

I considered for a few minutes why I wasn't able to just blow off this silly idea I had to take someone to dinner for my birthday. Why did I care so much if I was to let the idea go? The driver and Tommy were the only two people who knew I was on the island and neither thought anything of me. Why was I already creating guilt around my decisions?

I couldn't find an answer during the few minutes I offered to that train of thought. Instead I went to the bathroom to take a shower. It was hot on the island and a cool shower sounded refreshing.

I grabbed my white linen pants and a cream cotton shirt from my bag. It would have gone nicely with what Tommy was wearing had we been dining together. I needed a tan but other than that I looked island-ready. I spread out on the bed for a few minutes and watched the fan oscillate before falling into an unexpected sleep.

The poppy field was on a beach right at shoreline. The ocean waves arrived just as my mother warned me to fly away. I awoke from the dream just as a massive wave hit my feathered chest.

Since it was 7:58 p.m. I took the elevator back to the lobby. Off to the right of the lobby were a restaurant, a clothing boutique and a jewelry shop. Just in front of it Tommy stood with my taxi-driver.

Tommy was still impeccably put together with his white suit and no suggestion of a full day at work in the hot sunshine. My cabby had long shorts on and a Rastafarian shirt with two holes on the right shoulder. They both smiled when I walked out of the elevator. For a second I imagined how my twin was celebrating the first day of our 26th year on earth. I wondered if she had had any of the same struggles, which had driven me to this searching. I'd never asked her.

I explained to Tommy my wish to invite the young taxi driver to dinner. He looked at me funny while I explained it but obliged by interpreting my request.

I insisted he explain that it was an invitation for dinner and I was happy to pay the meter the whole time. I also wanted him to share that it was my way of saying thank you for the kindness I had encountered on my way to the island.

Could he make it clear to the young man please that if he didn't want to join me it was no problem whatsoever?

Tommy talked as the young man listened, smiled, looked at me then went back to listening. He didn't say a word, just walked over to me. We sat down at the first table that overlooked the massive sea. The sun had set and the temperature was perfect.

Tommy walked over with menus and I realized he was going to oversee this little dinner of mine. The waitress looked displeased at Tommy's involvement and stood in the back of the restaurant with her arms folded in front of her chest.

I ordered a Caesar salad and wood-fire baked cheese pizza. I hadn't seen items like that on a menu since California. My dinnermate ordered some sort of sea-filled soup.

I wanted to know his name but wasn't sure how to ask. I knew the little Mandarin I had a command of wasn't going to cut it. Instead we sat there smiling. It felt genuine and the minutes seem to graciously zip past. A gentle breeze arrived and made its way through the five-star lobby.

When dinner was served a live band started playing Bob Marley covers. I looked up to see if my date recognized the tunes. He had, and was grinning from ear to ear. I was so grateful. It felt like a treat from fate. Here this stranger and I sat divided by language and circumstance, and most of our lives' experiences, yet we could both enjoy Bob Marley and a meal.

He slurped his soup and wrapped up noodles from time to time around his chopsticks as he left his knife, fork and spoon untouched. I enjoyed the salad and the pizza.

The song "No Woman No Cry" came on and he moved his chair beside me so he could watch the band and listen. We smiled and enjoyed the music together.

Another hour or so passed before the band finished its last song. The entire time the driver and I seemed to do quite well connecting without words. I paid Tommy who in turn passed it along to the waitress still lingering in the back of the restaurant. No other patrons had arrived. Tommy walked up and spoke for a few minutes with my dinner date, then turned to me and said,

"Your driver wanted me to thank you. He said he'd never had a nicer dinner before. He wanted you to know that this was his first time to sit at a table where silverware was served."

"Tommy, please let him know how grateful I am."

As I walked back to the elevator I wondered why I filled all of my dinners with conversation. The young man and I had watched the sea. We pointed out the same things we saw and needed no words to have a wonderful, shared experience.

We listened to music we both knew and enjoyed. We smiled and laughed a little at the newness and slight awkwardness of the situation but we connected all the while. Words would have been a distraction. We were just experiencing the moment inside the company of each other. It felt liberating.

By the time I got to my room I was ready to sleep for days. I opened my pack and pulled out a worn t-shirt with Marilyn Monroe's face on it to wear to bed. I'd gotten used to traveling and had exactly the items I needed. Two incredibly soft t-shirts, a pair of jeans, a hooded sweatshirt, one long-sleeved t-shirt, a pair of linen pants, two dress shirts, a black dress and a black sarong.

Other than that I brought a large Ziploc bag with a toothbrush, toothpaste and dental floss. I always had a handful of books and my CD player with a dozen albums. Nothing else was needed that couldn't be picked up somewhere along the way.

Typically, I took the time to lay everything out in neat piles beside the bed but I was too tired. I just put on the t-shirt, splashed cold water on my face and went to sleep. I would unpack in the morning.

The poppy fields were bright yellow and everyone could fly. We were all birds -- my mother, my brother, my father, my sisters and I. We dipped and dove and played with the clouds like we were swimming in the ocean. No one talked. No one wanted to talk. We just flew around, together.

Safe to Swim

Leave room for love to come in.

A loud alarm rang me awake at 7 o'clock. The previous guest must have set it. I wished Tommy had known and shut it off before I arrived. He hadn't, so instead I lie there with my eyes open. I wanted to carry on flying for a while and instantly missed the sensation I'd felt in the dream.

I rolled over and called room service.

"Yes, a large pot of coffee please. No, only one mug is needed. Thank you."

Tommy showed up at my door a few minutes later. I had a feeling he'd taken it upon himself to see to it I was taken care of. I knew acting as an interpreter, a waiter and room service attendant were outside of his job description. Perhaps I had frightened him with my unorthodox birthday request the night before. I was grateful for his attention.

I shook off the last bit of my flying sensation and wandered out to the balcony for a long cup of hot coffee. The ocean was calm and I imagined the entire ecosystem beneath its glossy surface. It was an expansive system working in harmony for millions of years before humans arrived.

I drank the entire pot of coffee imagining the brightly-colored world just beneath the ripples. I felt like a swim. After eight months in Shanghai my skin was not used to the direct sunlight so I rang Tommy to see if they had sunscreen.

They did and Tommy brought it up to me. There were very few

guests at the hotel. I wondered why but didn't care enough to ask. I assumed it had to be more expensive than the exact same accommodations to the right or left of it because they were packed.

I liked the personal service I was receiving and had already taken the time to lay out my clothes and toiletries. I didn't feel like packing and moving for a couple hundred bucks. The hotel had its own little beach. I thought it was a funny way of putting it, as if they actually owned those grains of sand.

"Alexa go enjoy our private beach. There are only two couples out there now so it will be quiet just as you like."

I liked that Tommy thought I liked the quiet. I had been running from it my entire life, assuming that the quiet would reveal the truth about who I was, making it no longer deniable. But Tommy had watched my birthday dinner and seen the ease of it all and perhaps he was right. Perhaps I was getting more comfortable with myself.

"Are sharks out there?"

"Yes, of course. Well, not nearby the shore, if that's what you mean. It's safe to swim. No problem. No problem."

I took little comfort in Tommy's insistence that sharks were "no problem". I recalled the non-warning warning in Hong Kong too. Instead of a swim I settled into a large black lounge chair and opened up the Lee Child tale I'd been reading during the train ride.

On the Chinese Island I started each morning the same way. Where my old mental patterns held fear I inserted routines. Routines somehow preoccupied my thoughts and attention enough to push fear aside. At 7 o'clock the alarm went off. I hit snooze twice then ordered a large pot of coffee.

Tommy delivered it to my room and waited a few seconds to see if I needed sunscreen or a fresh towel. These were the tasks the hotel cleaning service would take care of at a moment's notice but he tended to instead.

I missed Da's attention and liked the minute or two I began each day at the end of Tommy's gaze. I always let the coffee sit for twenty minutes, as it filled the room with the smell of morning. I walked out to the balcony and practiced Tai Chi.

Afterward the coffee was lukewarm but the room smelled like a home and so it was worth popping it in the microwave for thirty seconds. It was the same routine each morning and I found it comforting to know how the minutes would transpire.

Once I'd polished off the pot of coffee I was ready for the beach. I took one or two novels depending on my mood. I needed time to think but couldn't be forced into it by lack of alternatives. Having reading options left thinking an option too.

Today was the last day I had prepaid for the hotel and wanted to consider what my next move was. I'd stayed in Shanghai for almost 8 months and spent the two weeks after a short visit to Hong Kong on this sun-drenched island.

Money was becoming a consideration. I put the Lee Child down beside me and looked out at the sea that had been so unforgiving just the week before. *What next?* Nova Scotia might have been the right answer after all.

Since I got to the island my conversations with God had changed. I was finding that with the routines and solitude, the negotiations had subsided. It didn't seem to matter if I was a lesbian if I was alone. I wasn't begging for forgiveness or asking to be changed. I stopped washing my hands incessantly and could sit for hours alone.

I stopped, for the first time in my life, perseverating on God's thoughts about me. I was alone. *How could God punish me for that?*

I grabbed from my memory the recent trip to Hainan. I recalled the little angel. I imagined he would be anywhere I might need him should life require it. I felt a wave of trust splash across my face and chest. Maybe the whole world does conspire to make your personal legend come true.

I'd head to Vietnam. Tommy was right. I was starting to really like the quiet.

Inside Saigon, Two Beers with Roo

When there is nothing left to pull you from the darkness, travel. Travel is the compass back to self. Travel is the path to our greatest parts. It longs for us when we are gone and accepts us completely upon our return, saying only, "What took you so long, friend?"

I got a cheap flight to Vietnam and landed in Saigon. They call it Ho Chi Minh City now, but I like the way the word Saigon feels in my mouth.

The air was thick when I got off the plane as if decades of war and oppression could be visibly dripping down the thin cheeks of the city. It felt very different than the face of Chinese communism I'd just left behind.

In Ho Chi Minh there were children wandering the streets selling cigarettes and playing cards. They seemed to peddle any item that provided permission to walk up to a stranger and ask for change. They wanted real change -- the kind that would bring a different life, but settled on coins from tourists.

Unlike in Hainan, Vietnam teemed with foreigners. On my flight I traveled with a group of Canadians. They each proudly carried their red maple leaf hand sewn into their carry-on packs.

I also noticed a sun-kissed woman in her twenties dressed in a tight v-neck white cotton shirt exposing her breasts. She had a pair of thin black-rimmed glasses on and worn blue jeans. I imagined she was from Central America but couldn't be sure.

She sat behind me on the flight with her Walkman playing the entire time. For a few minutes without noticing I wondered what she was listening to and then caught myself thinking about her, so stopped.

The flight was shorter than I expected. When we arrived I watched the Canadians pack up their items. Then I remembered to look for the woman in the white t-shirt. Most of us wore the look of traveling -- disheveled at the very least, tired. Not this woman. She seemed perfectly rested, as if this was the first leg of a short journey.

She seemed familiar with the place which intrigued me. Since, I had nowhere else to go, I followed her out of the airport to a street vendor selling coffee.

In Vietnamese she ordered an espresso. The language sounded so beautiful coming from her mouth. It was the sound of fluency in another tongue.

I waited a minute then ordered the same by pointing to the spot on the menu that she had. In doing so, I finally caught her attention and a smile.

Right before I could return a smile, I caught one of the Canadians pulling out his wallet across the street. A small Vietnamese girl was standing in front of him asking for change.

Without thinking twice, or even once for that matter, the overly-friendly man pulled a $20 dollar bill from his wallet that also donned a Canadian flag.

With cheeks filled with his own pride he handed the bill over to the girl. My heart began to race. It couldn't be a good decision to hand a small child her entire month's income (or more) in a single moment.

I left my espresso order and intrigue about the woman at the vendor's booth and slowly walked across the street. I snuck behind one of the t-shirt vendors' stations and followed the girl with my eyes as she turned down an alley. As my instincts had suspected something was wrong.

Three grungy-looking teenage boys immediately approached the child. They were dirty and united by the fearless look in their eyes.

They stood right over the little girl as I mentally prepared to help. I had no idea what I could do against three strong street boys but I prepared anyway. As I had suspected the generous man hadn't considered the incredible danger he was putting the child in.

The boys had witnessed the earlier exchange and demanded the money. Without a fight she handed over the twenty-dollar bill. She'd had it in her possession for less than two minutes. Once they let her go I wandered back to my espresso.

I was disappointed that the beautiful woman in the white t-shirt was gone. But now I was really hungry and fixed my thoughts on food instead.

French baguettes dangled from most of the restaurants' windows. Even with the heat and humidity a bowl of noodle soup and a baguette sounded good. I walked past a couple of vendors until I found a shop front that looked clean.

All the tables were empty but one. On it a large bowl of steaming Pho sat beside two baguettes. I pointed to the table to place my order. The woman behind the counter seemed to understand. Then I pulled out a new Lee Child book from my backpack. I desperately wanted to get lost in Jack Reacher for a while.

One page into the book I looked up and caught the white t-shirt emerge from the hallway bathroom. She looked over at me and smiled. I felt a familiar stir in my stomach. I had a chance to smile back this time.

The woman was more stunning than I remembered. She was tall and slender, and looked like she belonged in a movie. I glanced behind us to see if a camera crew was nearby. It wasn't. She grabbed her bowl and walked over to my table leaving her baguettes and belongings where they were.

"May I?" She offered with an elegant Spanish accent.

I smiled having guessed the origin of her beauty, correctly. "Sure."

"First time to Vietnam?"

"Yeah. Just got here from China."

"China. Now that's an adventure. Spent a year there in '98."

I was more curious than comfortable revealing this early in the conversation. Fortunately the waitress walked out with my bowl of *Pho* and one baguette. She had modified my order on her own. Apparently a girl my size doesn't eat two baguettes.

My table-mate offered in English that her name was Paola.

"Roo, my friends call me that."

Short for "Kangaroo" I thought but instead of asking I took a giant sip of soup. It was delicious and for a brief moment I wished we could just sit there as I had with the taxi driver on Hainan and enjoy one another's company without words. But, she was too beautiful to ask anything of.

Paola couldn't read my mind and asked how long I'd be in Vietnam.

"I know the right place to rent motorcycles if you plan to get one."

I wasn't sure I was up for making plans. I needed the freedom I had been chasing for the past few weeks. Plans might scare away the processing I needed to do. I had so many unsettled things to consider. I needed time alone.

I offered that I was in Vietnam to clear my head and I thought I'd find my way to a beachfront for a while. I shared with her this idea I had on the plane to spend some time alone.

"Oh, are you having some sort of existential crisis?"

I didn't respond and drank more of my soup. Then, with less volume than usual, I said, "No, well, I don't think so. I'm just taking a break from God."

"I'm not sure that's how it works, friend."

"I'm not either. I was just tired of being so afraid."

"Well, good luck with that. I let go of other people's angry god a long time ago. Found God on a journey in Australia not too long afterwards."

Who talks that way? I wanted more of her but now this was just another distraction. I noticed her white t-shirt pressed against her chest and felt a splash of warm rush through me. She seemed to be without a single care in the world. The longer she sat with me the more curious I grew. *Why was this beautiful woman traveling alone inside Southeast Asia?*

We sipped the last of our soups in quiet, aside from the street children who approached us with trading cards and cigarettes every few minutes. Paola took the chance each time to speak to the children in the Vietnamese she already knew, as she gently declined their products.

There wasn't anything pushy or forward about her. She seemed to be soaking up the moment without any other motive. I ordered a light beer in a bottle and Roo followed. There was something about the iced cold drink that made it feel cooler outside than it was.

We had a couple more while Paola talked about her pilgrimage in Australia. She revealed that the name "Roo" came from a long journey in the desert and a connection with a Joey. I thought of sitting in Amanda and William's living room in Shanghai not too long ago watching Priscilla Queen of the Desert.

A year ago I didn't know any of these people. I didn't know what China looked like or the salty taste of Hainan. I hadn't known the freeing sensation that accompanied getting on an airplane without a plan. I felt grateful and a little dizzy. I knew it was most likely the travel and the heat but I turned down the third beer.

When we walked out of the noodle shop Paola grabbed a Trishaw peddling by. She offered to give me a lift somewhere but I wasn't clear where I was headed yet. I declined and mentioned something about hoping to see her again -- *someday if the fates allowed it*. She smiled back just as she had all evening long.

I found a dirt-cheap room to rent for the night. A number "2" had been haphazardly etched in the door with something as dull as a butter knife. I didn't care. It had a fan that oscillated and the night's fee came with a breakfast from the restaurant. They wanted $5 a night so I paid for two nights and went upstairs.

It was far too hot to sleep so I thought about Paola for a while and found myself looking forward to seeing her again. From the brief stories she shared it felt like she too had fought to hold on to God -- in spite of His messengers.

I wondered why humans made it so difficult. God created everyone -- He was all of ours. *Why do we think He has favorites?*

I found Roo's confidence encouraging, thinking maybe this would all work out after all. I was starting to see the difference between God and all those who spoke on His behalf.

I had skipped the ritual of laying out my clothing having settled on only a one-night stay by the time I noticed the clicking sound the fan made. Things were very different than Hainan. There was a clicking fan and no Tommy to ring at dawn.

Morning Sweepers

*As with each breath
and every rose petal
and each raindrop
inside every creation
the whole of the cosmos exist.*

The sunrise in Saigon was more spectacular than I imagined. I didn't catch it rise above the giant ocean or along a golden field, it just peeked through the cracks in my shutters. Instantly I felt awake and went downstairs for breakfast. The coffee served was rich and filled with a sweet cream. When my eggs and baguette arrived I'd already finished the coffee and ordered a second one.

I considered roaming around to see if I could find Paola but the chances seemed dim. I noticed inside the restaurant there was an old wooden desk with brightly colored brochures on it. There was a laminated bus schedule against the far wall with 1999 in the corner. I couldn't imagine it could still be accurate. So, I walked over and sifted through the materials instead.

The soft-spoken woman who had checked me in the hostel the night before and prepared and served my meal this morning was now asking me if I wanted to buy a bus ticket somewhere. I was pretty sure I did.

There was a ticket to Hanoi the city at the top of the country. I bought that ticket but promised myself I'd stop whenever I felt the urge. Hanoi was hours away and I really hoped inspiration would strike at some point before then.

The only thing I knew about Hanoi -- and the whole country for that matter -- I'd learned from textbooks or gleaned from cardboard signs in the hands of men at stoplights back at home. It was hard to believe this beautiful place had been home to a war that took so many lives.

After breakfast and a long walk through Saigon I went back to the hostel where I'd stayed the night before. I liked knowing what the shape of the #2 looked like on my room door. I still yearned for familiarity which was difficult to find on the road.

The woman who had tended to my every need thus far was now assisting a European couple looking for a place to stay.

The couple had their "Lonely Planet" guides out and lightweight scarves wrapped in various places. The young man wore his muted colored scarf around his bicep. His girlfriend's scarf burst of colors and was wrapped around her head. I made a mental note to buy a scarf next time I saw one.

When I purchased my ticket to Hanoi the woman had instructed me to meet the bus in front of the hostel at 3 o'clock that afternoon.

So at about 2:45 p.m. I ordered the same sweet coffee from my morning, but over ice this time, then sat on the curb to wait. I always carried a copy of "The Alchemist" with me and it felt more compatible with my mood than the Lee Child action novel I was carrying.

I opened the book and the admittance forms to Pema Chödrön's monastery in Nova Scotia slipped out and hit my toes. I couldn't help but remember the night I'd met LeeAnn in Chico and how quickly my life had changed.

Here I was traveling in Vietnam alone, letting the breeze guide me. *How long had I been longing for freedom from my suffering? Would it ever end?*

Four and a half hours after 3 p.m. the bus finally arrived. I'd finished the Alchemist for the umpteenth time. I'd already learned in China that everything took its own time on this side of the ocean so the delays rarely bothered me anymore. Without holding the expectation that things should be on time there wasn't much to be disappointed about. Things were the way they were, there was no need to fight it.

I guardedly slid between the two rows of people who spilled into the aisle. Once we were all in a seat I heard the old bus take a gulp of diesel and start again. The moment we started moving I started to dream.

"Mui Ne. Mui Ne. Mui Ne."

I opened my eyes to the bus driver's announcement. "Mui Ne."

I looked outside and saw the mighty ocean. I didn't know where Mui Ne was on the map but this was the feeling I'd been hoping for. This was my stop.

I got out and took a breath of sea air in. I was going to stay until this ache I had been running from dissolved into something else or disappeared altogether.

That was the plan, anyways.

Somewhere in the Middle

There, resting at the edge of what we've always wanted, is what we needed all along.

I spent the next two months in Mui Ne, the first seven days of which I spent in absolute silence. By the time I found a place to stay and a bite to eat I had agreed to do it. I'd tried to talk myself out of it with compelling rationale but none of it stuck. I didn't care if I had no formal training in "being silent" -- I wanted to do it.

I still wanted God. I knew the only hope I had left was to find God in silence. After the past year on the road, listening and the previous 24 years of praying to Him I was more uncertain of His presence than ever before.

I would make room for Him in silence. I would show Him discipline and as much faith as I could wring from my tired and broken heart.

I found a nice hotel with single unit huts dotting the beachfront. There was air conditioning and running water. I didn't need a television and there wasn't Wi-Fi in the world yet. It wouldn't have mattered anyway as I didn't have a phone or a computer.

All correspondence with home was done through Internet cafes. I needed isolation. Although Shanghai was far from home it was plush with amenities. I needed something different. A silent retreat in Vietnam would be just that.

I'd never read about a silent retreat or how one might go about it. But, I'd studied the Dark Ages in school. I knew people retreated to faraway places to read, and study, and be with God. This was my dark ages. This was my time to finally show God I was serious.

I wasn't talking a lot now to begin with. I was renting hostels and buying bus tickets but I'd learned in China how to order food and find restrooms without words -- this would just solidify the silence. All I needed was a schedule.

Routines and lists had gotten me through my life so far. Rituals had made my move to Shanghai bearable. I needed the day broken down in manageable increments so I knew what to expect and how long to expect it. It would be similar to the way the kindergarten day was broken up.

I settled into my thatched hut and turned on the ceiling fan to make my list. I'd meditate six times a day: 4 a.m., 6 a.m., 10 a.m., 1 p.m., 4 p.m., 6 p.m. That was the schedule. I'd eat at 7 a.m. and 7 p.m. I'd take walks and swim when I felt I needed something to do. If I felt compelled to write, I would write. No obligation.

Once I felt confident the structure of my upcoming days was in place I jumped in the shower to cool off. It was much warmer in Vietnam than I expected. The west coast I was familiar with in North America came with a cool breeze. Not here. The sea breeze here felt like a hot burp from a stranger's mouth.

I pulled out of my backpack my favorite white t-shirt and a pair of baggy multi-colored shorts that I'd purchased from a street vendor in Saigon. The rest of the backpack I stacked into neat piles based on type of clothing. The stacks instantly made my hut feel familiar and I crawled on to the thin mattress and looked out across the ocean with matching calm.

Tomorrow I would start with silence. I considered notifying someone at the hotel about the whole thing, if nothing else, so I didn't appear to be rude. Also, I wanted them to know I wouldn't need anything but two bowls of soup a day. I'd like one in the morning and one at night.

I walked back to the lobby. There was a young man behind the counter with a floor fan bringing warm air on to him. He had a soft green cotton shirt on and the same light colored eyes. I bought a couple bottles of waters from him and asked about room service.

He notified me the kitchen opened at 6 a.m. but said I could pre-order the soup if I was certain that's what I wanted for my next week of meals. He recommended all sorts of fantastic seafood dishes but I had my mind settled on soup. I wanted simple. I wanted to limit distractions. I wanted God to arrive.

We agreed that the food would be delivered at 6:45 a.m. and 6:45 p.m. I sort of mentioned something under my breath about not talking for a few days but the young man looked back without a response. It seemed silly and complicated to share my plans for a week of silence with a stranger so I swallowed the end of the sentence before it fully emerged.

Each morning began the same way in Mui Ne. The sun rose from beneath the ocean's belly and the morning sweepers started their work. Everyone with any space of their own began their day by sweeping. I'd noticed the amount of sweeping that was done in China but this was on a whole new level.

My day started a couple hours before the sweeping. At 4 a.m. the tiny bell on my watch rang out. I splashed cold water on my face and made my way to the end of the bed where I'd folded an extra cotton sheet provided by the hotel on the floor. I sat there to meditate.

I sat just as Da had instructed, just as Thích Nhát Hānh had explained, with attention to my out breath. I sat just as I imagined Pema Chödrön and the Buddha before her. I sat and witnessed my mind dance as if it was a day-old butterfly caught in a sand storm. Still I sat. After my meditation I crawled back into bed until sunrise.

At 6 a.m., the soft bell went off again, and I started the water for tea. I'd borrowed a mug from the front desk that was thick with chips along its bottom. It felt like the right mug for my soul.

I used the small white coffeemaker provided by the hotel management to boil water, then filled my cup with jasmine tea and walked out to the little porch. I sat on the ground and sipped my tea.

The porch was no more than ten feet from the tiny grains of sand dissolving into the sea. I sat there with the ocean each morning for an hour as the morning stirred. The building beside my hotel had been there awhile and was still family-owned. From where I was looking it seemed a steady sea breeze from any direction might cause fatal damages to the structure but somehow it remained.

An elderly woman ran the place. She had a petite figure that seemed permanently bent over in the position of her morning, afternoon and evening ritual of sweeping. I wondered if she found a way to stretch out at night or if the question mark shape of her shell still remained as she laid in bed.

Chi started sweeping exactly ten minutes before dawn. It was as if she had an on-going competition with the sun each morning. She began sweeping the beachfront that snuggled up to her café. Row by row she swept away the debris the evening left behind. When she was finished each grain was arranged.

After the beachfront Chi swept the breeze-filled café that seated 20 or 25 guests and was usually empty. She swept every area, meticulously. She had very little, but you could sense that there was pride in taking great care of what she had. I thought of my father and the wisdom he shared with us as children. *It was important to take care of what we had.*

In my mind Chi's life seemed to hold a great secret. I didn't know what the secret was but there was simplicity to her life that seemed to leave her cheeks turned upward and her front teeth showing from happiness.

I spent my early mornings on the porch. I didn't read or write. I just sat there with my borrowed chipped mug from the front desk and the massive ocean's mouth as my view. I watched the fishermen return from their early morning hunt.

Once they hit the shore they tugged and pulled their thin wooden boats on to the sand and away from the tide's massive grip. The rewards from their early morning departure and the ocean's generosity dragged in nets thrown over their weathered backs.

At 6:45 a.m. on the dot my steaming bowl of soup arrived. I couldn't offer any words to the young man who dropped it by. I felt my mind yearning to speak to him so instead I lowered my eyes slightly and placed my palms together.

I sat on the porch again as I'd been taught from my readings, with my legs crossed like a pretzel, and brought all the attention to my soup. I thought of the water that made up the sweet spicy broth. I knew at some point during the billions of years of our earth's journey that water had been in the ocean, in the clouds, as part of another sentient being.

All things like the water were without beginning and end. I thought of each piece of meat and vegetable the same way. I realized the soup itself held life and death. I thought of my own death and wondered what thoughts I was still holding that brought such fear of it still. I tried to find them in my mind but couldn't. Instead, I went back to my gratitude for the water.

When I had finished with my soup I placed the bowl outside of my door and went back into my hut to read. For many hours I read. The only sound I heard was the fan oscillating the air throughout the room. I tried to hear the ocean but she was quiet.

I picked up the book Da and I'd been reading in Shanghai before I left. I flipped to the chapter about a woman named Dorothy. The author Sogyal Rinpoche tells a story of his student who is dying from cancer. My thoughts chased down an image of Mary Ann and I was upset her face wasn't clearer. I thought of her hands instead. She had unmistakably strong hands.

I could still see myself sitting in her hospital room, holding her hand the moment her heart stopped. Mary Ann, like the Dorothy that Rinpoche spoke of, faced death with such dignity and courage.

I tried to imagine what my mind would do with the knowledge of my last day. *Could I face it? Could I accept death? I'd been afraid of Hell as long as I could remember.*

I put the Tibetan Book of Living and Dying down. I still wanted someone else's words in my mind but Rinpoche spoke so directly about death that I found myself short of breath.

I knew my backpack was filled with other authors I'd purchased in Saigon from a young man. He had approached me on the street with a stack of books pressed against his spine.

"One book. One US dollar. You want some, Miss? All written in American. Special for you. "

I smiled. I didn't say anything, just waved him closer. The phrase, "Special for you," had become one of my favorite things to hear while on the road.

The young man patiently untied and restacked his books on the floor in front of me. He was careful with each one as if it was a friend. I felt that way about my books and wondered how much I could have in common with this stranger.

The covers of the books in his stack were faded and it was obvious that a home print shop had made the copies. I thought of the authors and wondered if they would care to be sold for a US dollar on the streets of Saigon, by a man who looked physically hungry, and to a woman who was starving for answers.

I perused the books as I finished a French baguette piled high with jam and butter. Plato. Aristotle. Aquinas. Descartes. Confucius. I'd chosen a dozen to buy that day, all of which I'd been carrying around ever since. I should have given him half the baguette instead.

But I clung to the belief that I'd read them eventually. Either way, I needed to know they were there. During the most difficult times in my life I'd turned to these men.

My seven days of silence would equate to approximately 800 waking minutes a day to fill without talking. I put Rinpoche down and picked up the Bible to read. It was one of only two books I carried with me that I hadn't picked up from the traveling book salesman.

I read to myself from the Book of Matthew.

"Teacher, which is the greatest commandment in the Law?"

Jesus replied: "'Love the Lord your God with all your heart and with all your soul and with all your mind.' This is the first and greatest commandment. And the second is like it: 'Love your neighbor as yourself.' All the Law and the Prophets hang on these two commandments."

I lowered the book for a moment and looked out to the sea. *If that was what Christ directed then why did I feel so unloved, and even worse, condemned and judged.*

Christ had offered that of all the Commandments, to love God and one another as God loves each of us, was the most important. This truth hit me as it never had before. He told us so clearly what was most important to God.

I laid there on my bed with my eyes fixed on the mighty ocean. If this was the truth than so many Christians had failed miserably with people like me. The Commandments they were told to hold above all the others had been pushed aside so that homosexuals could be denied God's unconditional love. My heart ached and so I tried to find my breath instead.

No wonder my instincts had been to let go of religion. My heart demanded I moved away from judgment and persecution. My instincts were to move toward love. This was what Christ asked of me.

I went outside for a walk. My train of thoughts was in full throttle again. I imagined Da beside me. I thought of Isabel's wisdom about the inherent shortfall in human understanding. I didn't want to blame anyone. I didn't want anger to guide the path of my healing. I wanted to move forward.

I passed Chi's place and its impeccably combed sand and continued along the shoreline. The water was warm and brushed against my feet from time to time. I called my attention to my steps, to the earth, to the sand and the sea and felt some of the hurt pass through. This must be the feeling of letting go. I didn't hear any words or messages from God as I walked. I suppose at first that's what I had expected.

Instead I felt my chest relax a bit and let more oxygen in. The more I relaxed, the more oxygen I took in and the brighter the colors and smells around me became. I realized if God was real, that being or non-being, was all around me. If I was made by God -- of God -- than God was in me. Then I should go inward to find a way to hear God.

I would not turn back to scripture. Reading was no different than speaking. It was a distraction from understanding what was happening inside of my heart, mind and soul. I wouldn't speak or read until the seven-day self-imposed retreat was over.

By the time I got back to my hut my soup was sitting outside the front door. I took a much longer walk than I'd planned. My face and back already tingled with the sensation too much sun leaves against the skin.

I picked up my soup and thought a "thank you" into the air. It still felt unnatural not to speak even if just saying words out loud without an audience. The soup was cold and seemed like the right temperature given the heat radiating from my skin.

After my meal I took a shower. I kept the water cooler than usual as a reminder to breathe deeply and to apologize to my skin. I'd been under the haze of China for too long. I'd forgotten the power of a sun undeterred by a thick gray layer of smog.

As I dried off all I could think of were the books I'd traveled with. Like anything, the moment I deny it, it temporarily consumes my mind. I know that the craving will make room for the calm so I stuck with it.

I grabbed Da's copy of the *Tibetan Book of Living and Dying* and the Bible from my bag and held them against my chest. They would be there in seven days. I could do this.

It seemed ludicrous that not talking out loud or reading would cause this much discomfort. I had no idea what distractions I had depended on to keep me looking out instead of in.

With a fresh sunburn I crawled into bed. I glanced up at the ceiling fan and watched it oscillate until I woke up in the blue poppy field.

"Mom. Dad. Is there a God?"

"Why, of course there is, darling."

"Well, does God love us?"

"Yes, very much."

"Then why does God allow such awful things to happen to us? Just last week so many of our family members died in that snowstorm. Why would God let it snow when it has always only rained before?"

"God does not see death as the end. So, there would be no reason for God to halt the snow and stop our brothers and sisters from dying."

"Death is not the end?"

"No, sweetheart. Death is someplace in the middle."

Into the Quiet

The sunburn was far worse than I realized. I woke up shivering. It seemed likely that I was running a fever too. I got up and drank a glass of water on the porch.

The moon looked like a leftover sliver of light from the night before. I couldn't see the ocean yet, but the sound it made against the quiet night was comforting.

In the darkness I tried to be mindful of my thoughts. They were there awaiting for me to notice.

Vietnam. I'm on the other side of the ocean.
This sunburn hurts.
What am I doing with this self-imposed silence?

Find your breath.
Breathe.
Just breathe.

Remember Da's teachings.

Do I really expect to hear God?
Who do I think I am?
Who is this, I am?

If I am listening, who is talking?
Which thought am I?

If I am this thought, where is the other thought coming from?
Relax.
There you go thinking.

Just find your breath.

The 4 a.m. alarm sounded so I shut it off and continued sitting. The eight months in Shanghai with Da had given me the discipline I now depended on to meditate. My mind bounced along its path but I could at least sit still with it.

As I sat there breathing and paying attention to my out-breath, memories of my recent dream in the poppy field continued to surface. I promised the part of my mind stirring up the dream that I would tend to it later, then I returned to my breath. It was getting easier to identify the thinking in my mind.

By 4:30 a.m. I was back in bed. I'd been up most of the night and I felt exhausted -- so tired that I slept through my 6 a.m. alarm and missed my breakfast delivery.

When I woke up Chi had combed her beachfront and had already served breakfast to foreigners passing through. It was nearly noon. It was hard to believe I'd slept through the morning. I quickly rationalized I'd been up the last two nights at 4 a.m. and my body needed time to adjust to this new spiritual practice.

As I sat there rationalizing I wondered why my mind felt compelled to come up with a story. Who was I rationalizing this too? Myself? God? It hadn't mattered that I slept until noon, no one knew, no one was watching, and if they had been -- who cared?

The need to constantly seek external approval, understanding and acceptance had followed me to China and now to Vietnam. I crawled to the end of my bed and crossed my legs to sit.

I forced myself to sit there and pay attention to my thoughts. As best as I could I just listened to them.

Okay, so I slept in, big deal. Right? Was it? From whose perspective am I considering things? I don't care that I slept in. Do I? What's that mean about me? Does it mean I'll never find the answers I am looking for?

My mind was always telling a story. It was as if two experiences were constantly unfolding in my brain, the actual experience and then my mind's interpretation of it.

I noticed that if it was a good story, I kept it. If it was bad, I tried to get rid of it. I was constantly searching for a narrative that provided refuge from my fear of death, my fear of life, my endless fears.

I sat at the end of my bed from noon until 5 p.m. I didn't eat my soup and decided not to get up to drink water; if I was going to find God than it would require discipline and self-restraint.

Every ten minutes I altered the direction of my knees underneath me. After three reconstructive knee surgeries it wasn't easy to sit like a cinnamon twist but pain was part of this. I was still rationalizing. My stomach was aching with hunger pains when there was a knock at my door.

It was probably supper. I untangled my legs and as I walked to the door I felt a tingling sensation crawl throughout my limbs. I assumed it was from the last position I was in and tried to make a mental note not to sit that way again. *Why was I punishing myself with meditation? This couldn't be The Way.*

I scanned my hut to see if I'd accidentally left the soup breakfast bowl inside. They would have been expecting to find it on the porch and when they didn't they would have knocked. The soup bowl was nowhere in sight. I left it outside when I'd decided I wasn't eating today.

As I walked to the door I glanced in the mirror to check my hair and face before opening it. I looked tired but the sunburn hid it well.

Roo looked amazing. She had replaced her white t-shirt and worn blue jeans with a thin beige cotton dress. The sun had endlessly kissed her dark complexion since I last saw her. I instantly felt like kissing her lips but instead paid attention to my thoughts.

I gasped for a breath of air when I saw her. She reached in her pocket and handed me a gift then wrapped her arms around me. She smelled like a spring breeze.

"I've been thinking about you."

I stood there without words unsure of what to do with my silence.

I hopped over to my bag and grabbed the book on top. It was the Bible. I flipped to the back cover and wrote hastily, "I am in the middle of seven days of silence."

She looked back down at my words and then directly into my eyes. "Wow. Ok. Seven days. So, what day are you on?"

I lifted up two fingers wishing it meant how many days I had left.

Roo carried a gentle smile as she sat down on the end of the bed.

Nothing seemed to disturb her peace. There didn't appear to be any judgment, good or bad, toward my silence. She didn't need anything from me. It was so obvious how different it was to be in the company of someone who relied on herself to get her needs met. It was seeing a part of me I'd lost long ago inside of someone else.

I filled my mug with water and handed it to her. She drank it slowly and then walked to the door. I fought my instincts to talk. I wanted to ask how she found me but it didn't seem to matter. I wanted to ask her to stay a while but felt myself needing that too. So, instead I let her leave.

She wrote at the end of my sentence in the Bible a cell phone number and then left. I decided I'd wait until I ended my silence to open her gift. It would act as an incentive if I needed one. I had no idea how long Roo would be in Mui Ne but I hoped to see her again. First, I needed to finish the silence I started two days before.

All that I Am

The next five days of silence were constructed one minute at a time. Unlike the sand that effortlessly slipped through my toes nothing about the time slipped by without work. It was difficult but I wasn't going back to my old life. I couldn't.

Most of my time was spent on the porch and in meditation or prayer. When I took walking breaks I fought my instincts to engage in conversation with hotel staff or the local children playing kickball on the beachfront.

I had grown accustomed to distracting myself with other people. My neighbor Chi wandered over numerous times to say "hello" while I was practicing Tai Chi but eventually realized I couldn't respond with anything more than a smile. She was already smiling back.

I was no longer sleeping deeply through the night so my alarm was unnecessary. I woke a few minutes before my 6 a.m. meditation and found my dreams to be more like extensions of my waking day than like escapes to distant places and feelings.

To my surprise, even with my struggles to be mindful, the sun managed to rise and set each day unaffected. The passage of time brought with it a new perspective. It was a reminder of impermanence, and revealed that no matter what thoughts or feelings I had, no matter how easy or painful my days were, all things carried on.

It was difficult to understand my thoughts but each day I grew more curious and less critical of what was happening in my mind.

This softening made way for a new level of curiosity. I started to see patterns and habits I'd never noticed before.

If I experienced the world (or at the very least if I interpreted my experiences through my thoughts) then I wanted to understand how those thoughts arrived and departed.

After dinner I sat down to journal what I was thinking. It was something I'd done for years and it felt as familiar as praying the gay away.

With so many hours dedicated to sitting on the porch with little changes in scenery it became obvious that my feelings were directly related to my thoughts.

No telephone calls or movies, no television programs or outside stories -- just the thoughts in my head to keep me entertained. I stared out at the sea and it was as if a thought arrived on an independent journey just passing through my mind.

I could see a path running through my head that started far off in one direction and carried on infinitely in the opposite direction. I'd never seen the path before now.

Thoughts (memories, worries, stories) were traveling along on their own journey and simply popped into my mind for a visit, then returned on their way. They weren't mine to keep. They weren't mine at all. If I clung to the traveling thought for a moment then a feeling emerged. If I let the traveling thought pass on through there were no feelings created.

The more I paid attention to the path the more I understood my mind's reaction to the thoughts. If the thought brought about something unknown in the future or something unpleasant from my past instantly a physical sensation of discomfort emerged. My hands became clammy and my heart raced. Sometimes I could find pain inside of my chest or a tightness of breath.

If it was a memory that stirred happy feelings then instantly my body relaxed. I let it in and gave it my attention. If it was a thought that brought pain, discomfort, or uncertainty, I pushed it away.

The more I sat the more I noticed my mind's process was always the same. First a thought arrived, then a feeling, then another thought and then another feeling, on and on, endlessly. This process continued until I interrupted it to return to my breath.

It was exhausting to pay attention to what was going on in there. But my curiosity sustained me. *What if my thoughts were responsible for my suffering and my suffering wasn't because I was gay?*

I had to find out.

Hour after hour, I sat. Sometimes I could sense that my thoughts were creating the map my feelings were following; at other times, it was far more intertwined. But, just as I watched the sea birds swoop down and snatch fish I spent all day and night watching my mind. Instinctively, I clung to joy and pushed away pain. I had to pay great attention to those reactions.

On my last evening of silence I decided not to eat or walk. I wanted as much time as possible within the quiet to meditate. I couldn't believe after how difficult it had been to be quiet at first, how by the end, I wanted to stretch out the final hours.

Chi had swept the evening debris left over from the tide and had already gone in for the night. I could tell from the darkening sky that the sun was getting sleepy. I sat on the porch and was considering all of the people I loved. I thought of all those I knew by name and all those I'd not met but still loved.

I thought of the millions of human lives that had come and gone. I thought of each creature on earth and the natural cycle of life and death.

Each and everything that lives eventually changes form. As I focused my breath on the sea it became clearer that all things live and die, and take on a new form. Once the water left the sea it joined the sand. Once a palm leaf fell from a tree it became part of the soil. Our bodies were no exception. Everything dies in one form to become another. It does not end.

Death was part of life. It was a natural and yet mysterious as birth. *Why had I spent my life so terrified of it?* I knew there was more to all of this than what I could understand through my thoughts. It was clear that understanding God was just like understanding life and death. It cannot be fully grasped but to fear it makes no sense.

I wandered out to the edge of the shore looking to the moon. I felt connected to its reflection. I removed my shirt and shorts and waded around in the water for quite some time. I had no reason to rush the last night of silence.

I am of God, as the Earth is of God; therefore I am of the Earth. I should not fear returning my body to it one day. There is no reason to fear death. There is no reason to fear God. There is no reason to fear being who I am. And, without that fear, I am free.

Around 1 a.m. I finally crawled out of the sea and into bed. I was as water wrinkled as a newborn. I didn't bother to rinse off in the shower, I wanted the ocean salt against my skin. I shut my eyes and without warning fell asleep.

"Mom, Dad. I understand."

"What darling? What do you understand?"

"I understand why you raised me like a flower even though I was a bluebird. With all of the changes in the seasons -- unexpected frosts and harsh days of summer, not to mention the unforgiving rainstorms -- life can be hard. You just didn't want it to be even more difficult."

"You're right daughter, we wanted life to be kind to you," they offered with sadness in their voices.

"Now that I know the truth about who I am, I can look back and understand why I felt so different. It was painful to pretend the sun and rain sustained me when my stomach ached for food. I suffered pretending to be a flower."

"Daughter, we tried to protect you. When we realized you were a little bird we thought it would be better to raise you like a flower. We thought the Creator wanted that from us since you were dropped in our field. We didn't know anything about raising a baby bird. But, we saw your suffering and we wanted it to end."

"I understand all of that now. I came back to tell you it was your love that sustained me when I left during the storm. When I was riddled with fear, when I lost all hope, I clung to your love. Your love saved me."

I wanted them to know I didn't blame them for the pain I went through. They had done the best they could. They had always shown me love.

"When I left home I searched for a way to become a blue poppy. I asked everyone I met for help. Some laughed at me while others cried when they saw my suffering. Still others tried to trick me for their own gain. But I learned so much from each of them."

"Who did you meet, sweet daughter? Please tell us these tales from far away."

"My first friend was the large maple tree I found shelter in the night of the big storm; that first night you told me about my wings. For many days and nights, long after the sun returned, the tree held me." I took a deep breath and then continued to tell them everything.

"I cried there. I cried there day and night. Maple let me stay in the hallowed hole inside of her chest. She knew I was hungry and offered little insects and treats from her branches. Just as you cared for me, Maple did too. Then one day I heard her voice. It was not a sound I had ever heard before. It was like a sound from deep inside the earth.

She said, 'You must go now and find other birds like you.'

'Are there really others like me?' I asked Maple, afraid and confused, not knowing what from my past I could trust anymore.

'Yes, just as your mother promised. You can find them if you fly north. My family is all along the way and you can stop and ask for help and food. They will give you shelter from bad weather or long dark nights.'

'But I don't want to be a bird. I've never wanted to be a bird. Nobody asked me. I would have told them. I want to be a blue poppy, please help me Maple. Can you please help me become a flower?'

'No more than I can become a mountain, friend. We are as the Creator made us. To fight that is to fight the Creator. You were given wings. This is a great gift many other creatures desire to have. It is a great gift from the Great Creator. Fly!'"

I moved closer to my parents as both of their hearts seemed heavy hearing about the night I left the poppy field.

"I flew for many days without asking any of Maple's family to support me. I wasn't ready to accept what she said about who I was. I was afraid her family would say something similar. I wanted different advice. I wanted to become a blue poppy and return to my family. So, I flew and flew. I didn't notice the beautiful earth below me, nor the expansive sky surrounding my wings. I didn't notice the sunrise or the breeze.

I just flew with my attention chained to my pain. My thoughts centered on finding a way to become a flower. I didn't stop to eat or sleep. When finally I grew too weak to continue on my journey, I fell hard to the earth and landed in a meadow."

My mother dropped her petals slightly towards the earth as I continued sharing.

"Where I collapsed a ladybug was napping on a long blade of grass in the afternoon light. For a brief moment I noticed the cool blades against my wings. It felt refreshing. I noticed the small breeze that wove in and out of the meadow. I took a deep breath and then went back to my desire to become a blue poppy.

'Hello. Is someone there?' The ladybug was looking in the other direction from where I'd landed.

She spun around quickly and said, 'Well, hello there. You startled me. I guess I dozed off. Well, with this sun and all, you can't blame me, can you? Why, who are you, little bird? How precious. Join me for a cup of sun-brewed water. It's that time, sun-brewed water time, right after my nap. Oh, pardon me, how rude, carrying on so. What was your name then?'

'Um, well, my old family called me Blu but they are not my family anymore. No one calls me anything now, I suppose.'

'Not your family anymore. Now don't be silly. Once a family, always a family, I say. Something bad happened, I can see that but don't worry. It will pass. It always passes. Trust me. I am old. I know -- nothing lasts forever. Nothing, not even the things we want to last, let alone the things we don't. I'll pour our drinks and you can think of what you'd like me to call you. By the way, my friends call me Chattie but I prefer Lady. Chattie makes no sense to me.'

It seemed so obvious. I just smiled nervously instead of responding. As Lady got our drinks together I thought of what I wanted to be called.

When she returned, I knew. 'Please call me Popi.'

'Sure, if that's what you'd like. I happen to like Blu. But Popi will do. It's just a name.'

I wanted to tell her that it was so much more than a name. It was the first time in a great while that I could be a poppy again. But, I didn't say anything. Instead she talked.

We sat there the whole day and she never stopped talking. She told me all sorts of tales about her life and her family. She explained how each of her brothers and sisters had left home on different adventures and that she missed them.

'No one's ever really gone if you keep them in your heart.'

It was a comforting thought -- the thought that we are always with the ones we love no matter the earthly circumstance. I thought of you, Mom and Dad."

My dad reached a petal toward me.

"Then what happened, honey?"

"Before night came I interrupted her, 'Lady. Lady. Sorry to interrupt. I'm very sorry. But I need to know if you can help me learn how to become a flower.'

'A flower. Oh, no no no. Not you. You are a precious bluebird. You will never be a flower stuck in the ground. You can fly, sweet Popi. If this is about all that family stuff, it is time to move on. No bird I have ever known has wanted to become a flower. Let that silly idea go.'

A part of me knew she was right but I couldn't just let go yet. I would've rather died than lose all of you. I waited until nightfall and flew away. Lady was still talking, in her sleep now, as I flew off.

I flew through the night. I was afraid of the dark but didn't know what else to do. I prayed to the Creator, just as I had been taught to as a child, but the Creator didn't respond. I felt so alone.

So I flew and flew and flew.

By the time the sun offered its first ray of light I was exhausted. The fear of the dark night and the strength to fly through it had taken all of the energy I had left.

The new day revealed a large pond just below and a forest off in the distance. There were distant chirps that sounded familiar but I wasn't sure why.

I steadied my legs to land by the pond when I spotted a large turtle waking up. I dropped in beside him. He didn't seem to notice me as he yawned and walked toward the water. I didn't want to waste another entire day listening to chatter so I asked him my question straight away. I needed answers.

'Excuse me, kind sir. Do you know how to become a flower?'

He looked at me unimpressed and in a far deeper voice than I expected, said, 'Who wants to know?'

'Uh, um, I do. That's it, just me.'

'Well, then, yes, of course I do. I know how to become a flower. Everyone knows that.'

Joy bubbled up from the deepest point within me and I started to stutter, 'Not me, sir. I don't know. I don't. Can you please tell me? I want to be a flower so badly, you see, but, but I'm not. I'm a bird. Can you help me, please?'

With a scrunched nose as if he just got a whiff of something dreadful he said, 'Do you see the other side of the pond over there? The side with large trees behind it, where there is vast shade and deep pools to swim in?'

'Yes, yes, sure I do. When I was flying earlier I saw it too.'

'Well, I've longed to get back there for decades now. The problem is that it would take me weeks to make it there now that I've grown so old. I'm afraid I can't risk it out in the open day at my age and at night something would surely kill me. I can't swim the distance needed to reach the other shore either, so I'm stuck here.

'Oh, I see.'

'If you can carry me to that side I will be glad to share with you the secret to becoming a flower.'

'Really? Great. Wonderful! Of course, I will. Let's go.'

'Settle down. Settle down. It will take us time to prepare', he explained.

'Ok, Ok'. I hadn't settled down; I was trembling with excitement. 'Then let's not waste time. Let's prepare. Whatever it takes to become a flower, I can do.'

I spent thirty days preparing with Tuttle. He had already designed a basket as if he had been waiting for me to arrive. Now we just needed to make it.

For many days and nights we constructed the basket by weaving twigs and pressing leaves inside the bottom. His plan was for me to carry a large branch in my mouth across the pond that held a twig-leaf basket carrying him inside."

I looked at my mom and her face revealed worry.

"It's okay, mom. We never made the journey."

"What happened?"

"Well, when we weren't sewing the basket or fetching the materials, Tuttle and I just hung around the pond. We swam a little, ate a little and rested. We didn't talk that much so it was very quiet and I had time to think. I started to get used to being a bird.

Finally, one afternoon Tuttle sauntered over to me. I knew he'd been trying to tell me something but I haven't pushed.

'This is serious. What I'm going to tell you. So I'd rather you not repeat it. Okay?"

'Okay Tuttle.' I didn't have anyone to tell it to. All those I loved were in the poppy field still.

'My brother, his wife Tibi, and the rest of my family live against those beautiful trees on the other side of the pond. I haven't seen them in 30 years.'

'But why Tuttle? Why are you here alone?'

'Because he betrayed me.'

'Who did, Tuttle?'

'My brother did. You see, I was supposed to marry Tibi. I was the eldest son and she was the most beautiful turtle in our village. Everyone knew we were to be married.'

'Did you love her, Tuttle?'

He paused and looked down. Then with a new face began again, 'Obviously, yes. Well, of course, she was beautiful. She was the most beautiful turtle in our land. She was to marry me -- that's the point, not love. But my brother stole her.

A neighboring village was in danger from outside predators. As the head of our army I had to take my troops to this war. We were gone much longer than we expected. Ten years to be exact. When I returned my brother and Tibi had married.'

'I'm sorry.'

'Oh, don't do that. Don't feel sorry for me.'

'I don't Tuttle. I'm just sorry you lost your family. I know what that feels like. But, all you have to do is forgive him to get your family back. I have to learn to become a flower.'

'Forgiveness is not an option.'

'But you are the only one suffering, Tuttle. When I fly I can see clearly across the pond. Your family is happy while you are here all alone. Maybe you can forgive them, Tuttle. Maybe it is time to let go of what you thought would be and accept what is.'

My own words, and the wisdom within them, pierced my heart.

I grabbed at my chest with my wings. I thought of Maple and Lady. I thought of all the nights I'd prayed to be something I wasn't.

Tuttle scowled at me. I knew I'd said too much. I didn't want to jeopardize gaining the knowledge about how to become a flower so I shut my mouth.

Two more months passed and by the time the basket was ready I couldn't take it anymore. I loved my friend but his anger was unbearable. I was concerned he wanted to travel over to the other side to cause his brother harm. I decided I was willing to risk losing the secret to becoming a flower if I could help my friend let go.

'Today is the day, is the day, is the day...' Tuttle sang as we put the final pieces of the basket in place.

I'd already flown the carrier across the pond many times without Tuttle during practice runs. I worked on my takeoffs and landings. I was ready. I knew I could sustain the weight of Tuttle in the basket as I'd practiced with it filled with rocks for months now. I was strong and my flight was the best it could be. But, I couldn't take him like this.

'Yes, Tuttle. Today is the day you can make a new home on the other side of the pond under the large trees and with plenty of sun and shade and food for a lifetime. But I cannot take you like this. I cannot fly you there with a heart filled with regret and anger. You are rotting on the inside and will not be able to enjoy life. Sam and Tibi are happy and you deserve to be happy too.'

'You will take me as I am or I will not tell you the secret to becoming a flower. You will die a bluebird and all alone,' Tuttle barked.

'That is okay. Every day I was here I learned more about my unique qualities as a bird. I learned how to take off and land. I learned how to dive into the pond for food and to cool off when the sunshine was hot. Although I still long to know the secret of becoming a blue poppy, so that I might return home, if I am to stay a bird, I know now I can be happy, as I am.'

Tuttle looked at me and then looked away. He slowly crawled to one of the only shady spots on the dry, rocky, lifeless side of the pond.

For three days Tuttle laid there. We did not speak. I continued to swim, eat and fly about as I waited for him. He didn't move, not even, to eat and drink from the pond. I thought he might die.

I learned to wait by paying attention to my breathing throughout the day. I learned to watch the pond and the sky and enjoy every moment as it arrived. I fell deeply in love with breathing in the world.

Late one night in the middle of my sleep I felt a push from the side.

'I'm going to swim across. I know my brother will sense my arrival and will find me in the pond.'

I listened as he continued, 'I will ask for his forgiveness and offer my own. You were right. I'm the only one suffering. Sam and Tibi were meant to be together. I never loved her. I was just too jealous to tell Sam the truth.

I made a mess of my family with the constant fighting and demanding everyone choose sides. When no one was willing to, I left and promised never to return. But I have suffered from this choice. I have wanted to return home but was too embarrassed. I was afraid they could not love me after the mistakes I made.

I realized when you were willing to give up the secret to becoming a flower that you really cared for me. If you love me perhaps my family can too.

But, Popi...'

I interrupted, 'I know they will love you, Tuttle. You are perfect just as you are. You are their family.'

Tuttle looked toward the earth and I sensed his shame.

'But, Popi...'

'I know, Tuttle. I know. There is no secret to becoming a flower, is there?'

'No. I'm so sorry, there isn't. My shell was filled with anger and pain when I met you. I lied to you to get what I wanted. I am so sorry.'

'It's ok, Tuttle. Go home now. It's time.'

I thought about the forest I'd been so curious about during the time I'd lived at the pond. I knew it was my turn to be brave. I heard little sounds coming from inside the trees. The sounds pulled at my heart. So, I went."

I was tired of sharing my adventure, even though I wanted my parents to know how the story ended. But I couldn't talk anymore tonight.

"I need to rest now, mom and dad."

"Of course, honey. We'll talk again tomorrow. We're just glad you are okay."

Long Forgotten Apology

My head and back flew forward without any clear instructions from me. I'd been in a deep sleep. I scanned my body with my eyes then jumped up and turned the light switch on. I scanned the room sensing something wasn't right, but everything appeared to be how I'd left it to enter my dreams. Still I sensed something was missing.

I caught a glimpse of my face in the mirror. The sun looked nice pressed against my skin. I felt rested. I was eating pretty well. I'd cleansed my body of all unnecessary distractions like sweets, and alcohol and nicotine. I'd removed television, music and books.

I was meditating many times a day now and resting my mind without strain. The absence of using my voice had allowed me to hear my thoughts so clearly. Things felt more in balance than ever before.

So what was this sensation? I looked down at my hands and then at my feet. I was intact. I closed my eyes and felt my heart pounding. I took a deep breath into my lungs. I was here. *But something felt different. Something was missing.*

I dropped my legs off the side of the bed and felt my feet against the cold wooden floors. I reached to open the top drawer in the dresser I rarely used. I moved aside the scarves and Saigon tee shirts I'd purchased as gifts for family and friends.

Just beneath the bright colored items rested the gift Roo had dropped off four days ago. My heart sped up thinking of her. It was an attraction I couldn't deny.

My passport leaned up against the box. Both of the items I was looking for were there. I picked up my worn-in navy blue USA issued document.

Then I wrapped my palm and fingers around the gift from Paola. I wanted to open it right away. It was hard to imagine that I'd waited all these days, because all of a sudden I couldn't wait a second longer.

The ocean was restless and the cool air slipping through the windows caught my attention. I walked out to my favorite spot on the porch and sat down. I felt safe. I took a few deep breaths and relaxed. The box was wrapped in a piece of cloth. I untied the rope that held the cloth around the box. I placed the fabric and the twine beside me and then looked back to the ocean. There was no need to rush now, I was opening it.

Inside the box rested a thin brown leather necklace with a tiny glass bottle dangling from the end. A snapshot of the first time I saw Roo in the airplane popped into mind. The leather necklace had been around her sun-soaked neck. When I asked the significance of an empty bottle around her neck, Roo graciously explained that it was not empty, it was filled with her truth.

There was a short handwritten note folded and stuffed at the bottom of the box. I opened it slowly as if I'd been waiting for this letter for as long as I could remember.

The word "Today" was written where most people would feel drawn to include a date.

Today.

Alexa Leigh,

Seek your truth. Seek only your truth. In the gentle light of day or within the long stormy nights, chase it with every inhale and exhale you possess. For God is there. God has always been there. God is there loving you -- just as you are.

Roo

I gently placed the necklace and the note on the end of the bed. I'd been on this path since as long as I could recall. I wanted to move toward love and liberate my heart from fear. I sought my truth and Roo had seen that inside of me. *Why else would she have offered me these words and this symbol of understanding?*

I crawled to one of my sitting spots in front of the window. As I sat there I realized the pain I'd carried my entire life -- because I was ashamed of being gay -- was gone. The angst, the shame I'd had in the pit of my stomach every morning when I woke up, for as long as I could remember, *was gone*.

I took in a huge breath of air and let a million old thoughts leave my mind. I understood now that they were never in my heart to begin with.

This was my moment of truth. This was what I had crossed the ocean for. I held my arms across my chest then looked in the mirror and said, out loud and with a voice I'd hadn't used in days, *"I am sorry. I am so very sorry. Please forgive me."*

For the first time in my life I wasn't talking to God. I was talking to the part of me I'd spent a lifetime rejecting. I was ready to accept who I was and let go of the pain from my past. The hurt and anger was gone.

With the moon peeking through my window, I finally understood, that loving who I was, without all of the fear, was the only way to know the God who created me. It was also the only way to truly offer love and acceptance to others.

I spent the next month and a half in Vietnam. I never saw Roo again. That was the nature of life on the road. Traveling alone seemed to make connections more profound and undeniably temporary. I suppose all earthly relationships are, but travel exaggerates this reality.

I thought of Roo often and read her words each night before I went to sleep. I knew the words by heart but liked the way her gentle brown hands pressed letters into the paper. She had seen in me all the work I'd been doing.

Chi and I found each other at dawn and with few words in common we sipped on the silence and enjoyed each other's company. I sensed her peace with life and with God.

I wandered around the village and felt a connection to each person I passed by. I understood now that we were all made from the same source. We all desired to be loved and to love. And, in the end we all spend many hours of each day working through the thoughts passing through our mind.

Every day I carried on with my meditation and Tai Chi. I was learning a great deal about myself and found the practice of acceptance so rewarding. I was disciplined. I needed very little and watched my body take a smaller form to adapt to my behavior.

I continued reading and studying. My meditation practice grew to reach different parts of my day. Thích Nhát Hānh guided me. I practiced leaning into the groundlessness that Pema Chödrön mastered. I was calm. I found forgiveness in my heart and I began to understand how right Roo was -- God was waiting wherever I was.

But things in my life were about to change. Things always do. This life, wandering and alone, inside a hut dotting a beach somewhere in Southeast Asia was not going to be the rest of my life. This solitude was about to end.

The money I'd saved from the kindergarten was nearly gone and I hadn't looked beyond my evening bowl of soup for two months. *I had found some peace alone but how would I survive when all of the silence was gone?*

Land of the Eternal Spring

"Hillary. Hill. Hi, it's Lex."

I didn't feel like a 'Lex' anymore but had defaulted to the past.

"Lex. Hey girl! How the heck are ya? We miss you around here. You home?"

I was sitting in a quiet Internet café in Mui Ne with an iced Vietnamese coffee sweating on the table the rotary phone was resting on. I'd left the beachfront hotel and had a long goodbye with Chi.

We didn't talk, we just sat on her freshly swept beachfront and watched the ocean come in and out. I felt connected to her and knew it was all as it should be.

"Lex, you there? How the heck are you? You've been gone forever."

For a moment I questioned whether or not I'd been gone at all. When I heard Hill's voice the memories of sitting on her couch riddled with fear came flooding back. I could smell the thick Chico heat. I could taste the shame. I shook my head and took a huge gulp of air. *I wasn't still afraid, not like before, was I? Could my memories take me back to that place in my mind?*

The caffeine started to kick in and as Hill continued talking I realized I needed to take much smaller steps where my past was concerned. I put the coffee down and ordered a mint tea.

"I'm not sure Chico is home anymore," I offered reluctantly.

"Where to then?" We both paused for a while and I hoped she

thought it was a delay due to the seas between us.

"Honestly, I have no idea. I've spent the past couple months in Vietnam but my money is about out and I need to find a job."

The conversation felt so North American yet undeniably accurate. I needed work. I needed money to live. I recalled a conversation I had in Shanghai with Amanda when she explained only Americans start a conversation with a perfect stranger by asking, "So what do you do?" Still, I needed an answer to that question.

"Oh, you're looking for work? Well your old boss Brian, Brian Martin, called a few days ago. He was trying to find you. He had no idea you were in Asia."

"Did he leave a number?"

"Sure did. Hold on, I'll grab it."

I'd met Brian one summer during college and whenever I needed extra cash he had work for me. He was spiritual but despised religion and I suppose I craved his honesty.

Hill came back on the line and read me his number. He was still living in Chico as revealed in the first three digits of his landline. I finished up my call with her, grateful to be reminded of the one person in the world I could always depend on for work.

The last thing I felt like doing was heading back to the States but my options were limited, so I rang Brian.

"Mr. Martin!"

"Leeeeeeex. How the hell are you sweetheart?"

"It's been a crazy year but I've enjoyed it. I'm calling from Vietnam."

"Viet-fucking-nam. Wow! I love the universe, Lex. Really I do. I was just thinking about you. I called you in fact."

It didn't occur to Brian that I knew this information. He lived in the present moment making that thought unlikely.

"I'm heading with friends to a place called Antigua. Antigua, Guatemala. I'm not sure I'm ever coming back. It's a long story, credit card problems, won't bore you with details, but you should come. Can you make your way to Latin America? There will be work there."

No words had ever sounded so good. I was ready to work for others after all of these weeks of working on myself. I felt quiet on the inside but I knew from past experience that life would get complicated soon if I didn't have something meaningful to do. I needed a purpose. I swallowed the majority of my excitement as I let a reserved "yes" escape my lips.

There wasn't anyone else to tell but my family and I knew they would worry so I decided on calling them once I was safe in Latin America. First, I needed to find Guatemala on a map and figure out how to get there with the money I had left.

"Where are you?" Brian asked over a scratchy phone connection.

"Guatemala City!"

"Oh, I'm sorry, sis. My plans have changed. I'm heading to Belize instead but not for a while."

"A while?"

"A year or two."

I got off the pay phone outside the Guatemala City Airport. I'd gotten used to meandering between my expectations and reality. It was a comfortable temperature for uncertainty so I removed the beige sweater I always wore while traveling and sat on a bench.

Cars were zipping in and out of the airport lanes that wrapped around the terminal. I could feel the West around me. I hailed a cab and asked in English for a ride to Antigua. The slightly underweight man nodded in understanding.

If I possessed more Spanish than what I'd gleaned in eleventh grade I would've asked him a few questions during our short journey. Instead I was quiet and spent the time concentrating on my breath. I loved finding it throughout the day. It was always waiting for me to remember it.

Before I hung up with Brian he'd given me the name and contact information of his friends in Antigua. He was certain their little macadamia nut farm needed helping hands. I had two to offer and didn't let the uncertainty of it all bother me much. I was getting used to uncertainty and enjoyed its predictability. I knew Da would be proud.

It didn't take long to get to Antigua. I fell asleep for a little while but the trip was less than an hour so there was no time to dream. The taxicab driver cleared his throat to wake me just as the paved road turned to cobblestone. He pulled up alongside what looked like the town square.

Brightly dressed women and their children were wandering around the square. A fountain acted as the perfect centerpiece. A young man sat on a bench strumming his guitar. A half a dozen travelers walked around.

A tall black man, with black cowboy boots and a matching cowboy hat, caught my attention. His face looked much younger than his walk suggested.

I paid the driver with my newly exchanged currency then propped my large backpack against my spine and walked toward the fountain. I kept my eye on the cowboy.

I plopped down on a bench beside the guitarist and spent an hour listening to the new sounds of Antigua. The sun started to set. The yellows and oranges made everything feel safe. The cobblestone road wrapping around the town square made me feel like I was in a decade long before now. I touched the calm I found in Mui Ne resting inside of me.

The man in boots walked around the foundation. Mindfulness. I knew now what it looked like on someone's face. I watched the sun kiss the tops of the three volcanoes good night. The volcanoes -- Agua, Fuego and Acatenango -- acted as a backdrop to my new adventure. It felt majestic and there was a mandatory sense of humility and surrender to be anywhere that nearby an eruption.

I wasn't afraid. Unlike all the other times I arrived in a foreign land this time I carried less anxiety in my chest. I sat on the bench until long after sunset and then the man with boots walked over to me.

"You just arrive?" His rich African accent drenched each English word, making it sound like the first time I'd heard it.

"I'm Godwin." He continued, "Welcome to Antigua!"

I didn't know then how small Antigua was. It was like any other small town. Everyone seemed to know each other. The indigenous, the Spanish, the ex-patriots, and those just passing through were vibrantly recognizable from each other after just a couple days in the town.

"Is there a good place to eat around here?" I asked.

"Oh, sister, welcome to the land of the eternal spring -- where bakeries and cafes greet you any time of the day and tortilla soup tastes as it did for the very first person who ever prepared it."

I loved the way he spoke.

"I can get used to that," I offered through my smile. I resisted the urge to ask him what he did and instead said, "Is there a place to Salsa?"

I'd read in my "Lonely Planet" that people make their way to Antigua to study Spanish and salsa.

Everything in Antigua was connected. I discovered this very quickly. The locals and foreigners alike talk about the city's geographic placement on the globe and its energy fields. I didn't know anything about how "energy" worked but watched how everything seemed to point to serendipity.

As it turned out, Godwin was a 28-year-old Nigerian doctor who had been hired to work for the farmers Brian had sent me to find.

I was there to take Godwin's place on the farm. As it turned out, Godwin had left the job once he realized it was not the opportunity to help the indigenous people that he had expected.

"It wasn't what it appeared, sis."

Godwin never spent time on gossip or negativity when there were great issues in the world to resolve. I didn't press him on it but instead decided I'd trust him and find work elsewhere.

In the meantime, I studied the doctor's work. He traveled to remote villages and put on health-care clinics for the indigenous. He worked with the World Health Organization and various other nongovernmental agencies.

When Godwin was back in Antigua he volunteered at a children's hospital by day and spent his evening soaking up the little Latin town. It was a like a life out of a movie and I was grateful to be allowed in.

On our walk home from that day at the children's hospital I asked Godwin why he gave the little free time he had to the orphans at the hospital.

"I go there to hold the babies. I go there so they know they are loved. This is what God has asked of me. Do you know yet sister, what

He has asked of you?"

I no longer believed in anthropomorphizing God but I understood what Godwin was asking. I knew now that God had a million names.

"I'm afraid not. I know that I feel closer to myself when I am working beside you than any other time in my life. Your work breathes oxygen directly into my lungs."

"Then, perhaps, you know after all."

We walked for a few hours inside the quiet night. I let his faith in God's plan for me rest against my heart. I had no idea what that felt like but I was starting to see that this work brought me comfort.

Godwin believed the message of Christ was about the way we served and loved one another. The idea of earning salvation was not to be considered. The idea of using fear, rules or judgment missed the core of Christ's message. And, of course, he never denied anyone the right to know God's love. Godwin honored his faith with his life -- his service.

He needed no more than a few dollars a day to survive and dedicated his life to providing health care to people with the greatest needs. He didn't ask if they deserved it. He didn't want the responsibility of deciding who was worthy or not of healing. He lived modestly and spent what he had on the poor.

It was an illustration of Christ I could wrap my heart around. I finally understood what Isabel meant when she said that God and religion were not the same thing. I wanted to know every detail of Godwin's journey and how he got from Nigeria to Antigua. He didn't reveal it overnight but in time he graciously offered the stories that made up his life.

Godwin lived in a rural Guatemalan village a few chicken stops from Antigua. It was cheaper rent and provided the quiet he needed after long stints in the field. He talked about the landscape and the community as if it was home.

He understood the long and complicated relationship between the indigenous and the Spanish. He offered what he knew about topics I'd never even considered thinking about. He spoke fluent Spanish and could communicate in many of the tribal dialects.

"My mission is to alleviate the suffering of all those I can. It is my service that matters, as I have learned the outcome of my work is solely based on the will of God."

I'd never known anyone who carried a personal mission statement, certainly not one that was dedicated to helping those in need. It was a calling that resonated with every cell in my body. It was the piece of my life I still did not understand. *What could I offer the world?*

I thought about the past year of my life and my journey toward self-acceptance; my journey to find peace with God. I was ready to offer some of the love I'd found alive in my heart to others. I knew now that humanitarian work was the reason I cleared the fear out.

As often as I could I worked alongside Godwin. Weeks spilled into months and the rainy season came and went. With good weather it meant Godwin would be taking his work on the road. Although I rented a flat along one of the charming streets of Antigua I preferred his rural setting and asked if I could stay at his place when he was on the road.

The pace of life in Guatemala was similar to what I'd grown accustomed to on the other side of the Pacific Ocean. I remained vigilant to my rituals and found solace in taking care of myself.

I was filled with curiosity and happiness. I needed very little money to survive and found work easy to come by. Once word got out that I could help raise funds from America my cell phone never stopped ringing.

Without the constant fear of my own death and God's wrath, I had time to soak up Latin America and dive into humanitarian work. I was serving. I was serving and receiving in abundance. I had purpose.

Godwin invited me many times to assist him on the trail. I experienced with my own eyes the vast challenges so many humans face from the moment they inhale their first breath.

Unlike in Vietnam, in Guatemala my thoughts were focused on the wellness of others. I learned to fix my mind on healing and peace. I used Da's techniques and found I could spend many hours each day in meditation and prayer.

"I'm leaving in the morning. If you want my flat, it's all yours." Godwin offered over the phone line. I was sitting in a little café in

Antigua sipping tea.

"How long will you be gone?"

"Hard to say, Lex. I have a patient that lives in the hills and if the water is high or rocks have fallen it could take weeks to get to her. Rosa. Sweet Rosa is her name."

"I'd love to crash at your place. I'm working on a new short story and could use the solitude. I will keep you in my prayers."

I hung up my new cell phone by flipping it closed. It was late in December and I assumed Godwin would be gone until after the New Year. I decided I'd spend my days writing about my experiences in Antigua. I'd give the rest of my time to the children's hospital.

With the beautiful example of Godwin's life in front of me, I stopped questioning if God loved me, and instead spent my time doing the things I imagined the Creator of all of life, would love.

The answers which seemed so important when I left America faded into the daily grind of serving others.

You Can Find Me There
When the Third Way Appeared

It was dark when I woke up. I loved being awake before the world stirred. It felt like the time when secrets from the universe were shared. I also wanted to get an early start on a story I had in mind. I was writing four to five hours a day now.

Godwin's place was in an old rectangular shaped concrete building with a long flat roof. I climbed a metal staircase up the backside of the building and greeted the sunrise with a breathing practice I'd come to cherish.

Although I was no longer waking up in the middle of the night to meditate I did start and end each day that way. I was becoming more familiar with the practice of bringing awareness to my minutes all day long too. When I walked. When I cooked. When I did the dishes -- I used my breath to keep my mind on the present moment.

Some mornings I included Tai Chi, but not today. As I sat on the roof I listened to the neighbors' roosters greet the day. I knew each of them and their following of hens would spend the entire day pecking at the earth for food. It reminded me that I needed to head into Antigua to go grocery shopping.

So after the sun was completely above my head, I crawled down the roof staircase and back into Godwin's space. I noticed, as I had so many time before, how tiny and in order everything was.

Paintings and colorful Mayan masks decorated the walls and revealed Godwin's time in this land. I felt safe and contemplated asking

Godwin if I could stay there even after his return. There was plenty of room and I wouldn't mind having a roommate again. I'd lived alone since the French Concession. I let the thought linger for a while as I showered and got ready to head into town.

I knew the walk to the chicken bus stop was short because I'd taken it numerous times. I didn't see a single soul as I passed by the town square and brightly-painted Catholic Church. I sipped on a cup of tea from Godwin's place and gave more thought to asking him if I could move in.

Then, I saw the face holding the machete. It was as cold and round as the moon.

I know now that things slow down in moments of shock. The brain must process differently with adrenaline racing through the veins. The stranger and I stood there connected by the blade of his machete against my neck and the matching chocolate brown of our eyes.

We exchanged movements. It was a dance I'd never seen before nor imagined I could know. Yet, somehow I knew what to do. Move. Move. Keep moving. There was a voice, emerging from deep within me, telling me to freeze but somehow I knew not to trust it. I kept moving.

Who will call my parents? It was the thought that proved death was near. I felt a warm sensation drip down my spine. Then, a chill took over me as I stood there in the bright Latin morning light. I dropped my backpack. What was the value of anything save oxygen in a moment like this?

Certainly, a part of me assumed that offering my belongings to this stranger would conclude our dance. But I stepped away and he stepped toward me. What could he want now? Everything of value was there, offered, no questions asked. Sure, I had been startled at first but I rallied quickly. I had done my part. I was a guest in his land and made my offering.

Adrenaline tore through my unprepared vessels. It was like waking from a nightmare with heart pounding but instead of the overwhelming relief that follows the realization of a dream this time adrenaline ensued. It wasn't a dream. Fight or flight. But how could I do either?

Then, out of nowhere right in the middle of my shock a blue and battered Toyota pickup truck came bouncing along the dirt hillside. The stranger with the round face pulled back, as he knew seconds before I had that his window had closed. The truck was the local police. Was this the normal time they came skipping down the dirt road?

The two officers had seen me. They would certainly help. The man with *chocolate brown eyes had already grabbed my bag. I suppose he was not willing to lose the battle completely. He jumped on his bike and peddled straight into the bright green forest.*

Within seconds the police officers pulled up. Without even a nod in my direction they jumped out of the truck, brandished their pistols, and ran into the woods. The cheerful truck was left running beside me. The silence in the cool forest was pierced with gunshots. I fell to my knees to pray. I wasn't sure what I should say, but I wanted the boy to escape their bullets.

There is no way to tell how much time passed, but eventually the officers walked out of the rain forest with a beat-up purple bike and a pair of worn Nike running shoes in their hands. They helped me into the truck. I sat squeezed in between them as we drove around San Lorenzo el Cubo looking for a man without sneakers on. This was like looking for a raindrop in the ocean.

A few hours later the officers dropped me off in Antigua. It was where the retired yellow North American school bus would have carried me that morning had I taken a longer shower or sipped a second cup of Nescafé at Godwin's house. I hadn't and it hadn't. Instead, it was these young officers who'd saved my life.

I walked slowly to a bench near the foundation. The volcanoes holding the old city looked closer than I remembered them being. The air felt fresh. The young man who was always there strumming his guitar was playing.

I sat there for quite some time and felt connected to everyone and everything around me. Life felt more precious than I'd ever imagined. Death had come close and then left again. I was not afraid.

I walked to my flat a few blocks from the town square and crawled into bed. When sleep arrived I was already in the sky.

Flying.

The forest was a brilliant green. The song of the birds that I'd heard all that time by the pond with Tuttle seemed to soften as I approached.

Sunlight was casting through the trees and creating pools of light on the mossy, moist ground. It was so easy to breathe. I found a spot below a large maple tree and decided to rest a bit.

I spent a moment reflecting on my journey through the world

since I had learned to use my wings. For the first time, I didn't long to be a flower anymore.

I knew who I was and felt content.

"Hello."

I looked around the base of the massive tree and saw a bird covered in orange feathers in front of me.

I felt my heart start to race as I managed to let a word escape. "Hello!"

"Are you new to the forest?"

She was stunning and it took me a moment to find words.

"I'm not sure. It feels so familiar."

Then the beautiful orange-feathered bird walked up close enough to brush her feathers against mine, and my heart leapt.

I woke up a couple hours before dawn. It took me a few seconds to figure out where I was. The dream felt so real I looked around expecting to see trees. I knew what the dream meant. It was time to go home.

I reached for the lamp beside the bed and turned it on. It revealed a room I'd spent almost no time in. There was a stack of books beneath the lamp that I imagined I'd read but hadn't yet.

I noticed the piece of cloth that Roo used to wrap the necklace in sticking out of one of the books. I'd forgotten I was using it as a bookmark. I grabbed it and held it in my hand to remember those days in Vietnam. Then I wrapped a sweater around my shoulders and crawled to a spot at the foot of my bed.

I knew finding the space between my thoughts would comfort me more than anything else. I sat with my legs crossed until eventually the morning light covered every part of the room.

As I sat there preparing to go home I realized that I'd always had a choice to make. It was not, as I'd so painfully imagined all of these years, about my sexuality. Nor was it about my faith in God. My sexuality and my faith were no more a choice than the color of my eyes or sound of my voice. Neither could be changed or taken away.

It was a choice to be guided by love or by fear. They were not the same path. That was the choice. It seemed so simple when I said it in my mind but it had taken me so long to understand.

I walked outside and gulped the new morning's air into my lungs. I was so grateful to be alive. I prayed for the young man I'd encountered on the hillside just the morning before. I prayed for everyone I'd met along the way and all those I held in my heart with distance between us.

Each of them had helped guide me to my truth. God was love. I felt gratitude push to the corner of my eyes. There was a peace in the moment I could hardly comprehend, and so I didn't try. I let all the words in my mind leave and found my breath instead.

THE END